SIDE ROADS

Excursions into Wisconsin's Past

SIDE ROADS

Excursions into Wisconsin's Past

By FRED L. HOLMES

With drawings by Dorthy E. Meeker

1949

The State Historical Society of Wisconsin

MADISON

Printed in the United States of America

Preface

With the passing of Fred L. Holmes, Wisconsin lost its favorite storyteller. No other's pen has more successfully recaptured and saved for posterity many of the more romantic and colorful aspects of Wisconsin past and present. Lawyer, journalist, politician, and historian, he acquired through his wide contacts, genial personality, and insatiable curiosity a host of friends and an encyclopedic knowledge of little-known aspects of his native state. In earlier books he has brought to life its peoples and its scenic beauties and has given us sketches of its leaders which in their depth and richness testify to his intuitive understanding of his fellow men. In this book he turns to scenes familiar to his generation and its predecessor, to a period with an atmosphere and flavor all its own, which a considerate fate sandwiched between the age of homespun and backache and the day of the security state.

It is fitting that this, his final book, should appear over the imprimatur of the State Historical Society of Wisconsin, which he loved and served as an active, faithful, and useful member of its board during the last decade of his life. The essays it contains, which were offered the Society for publication by his sister-in-law, Miss Margaret Pollock, were part of a larger project which was halted by his untimely death in 1946. For many readers they will stir nostalgic memories not only of the scenes so skillfully recreated but of their delightful and charming author, who will long continue to live among us through the pages of his books.

Publication of an unfinished manuscript is inevitably somewhat unfair both to the author and to others. The thing that

v

would have hurt Fred Holmes most is the omission of some acknowledgments that should be included. Notes attached to his manuscript indicate his desire to express his appreciation to Thomas W. Brahany of Washington, D.C., for a copy of the dance program mentioned on page 48; to the late Colonel John J. Hannan, Milwaukee representative of the *Chicago Tribune* at the turn of the century, Oliver E. Remey, formerly editor of the *Milwaukee Free Press,* and William T. Evjue, editor of the *Capital Times* of Madison, for their contributions to his sketch of Milwaukee saloons and beer gardens; to Leo E. Vaudreuil, Kenosha attorney, for his memories of the first ice cream "Sundays" served in Two Rivers during his boyhood; to Ida P. Richards of Baraboo for her reminiscences of early Christmas celebrations, embodied in the letter quoted on page 112; and to S. L. Foote, traffic manager of Oscar Mayer and Company of Madison, L. L. Lamb, Madison agent of the Illinois Central, and representatives of the North Western Railroad and the Chicago, Milwaukee and St. Paul for data pertaining to the shipments of natural ice during the heyday of the industry. Thanks are also due Albert M. Fuller, botanist of the Milwaukee Public Museum, for data supplied on the flora of Wisconsin. It is probable that still others gave information to the author, but unfortunately their names are lost to us.

Turn now to the "Side Roads" that Fred Holmes opens up and let them lead you back to an earlier day. For many of you his rollicking stories and colorful vignettes will stir recollections of things all but forgotten, recreating them with a flash of vividness that obliterates time and makes them seem like yesterday's experiences.

CLIFFORD L. LORD

State Historical Society of Wisconsin
1 September 1949

Contents

GRANDMOTHER'S FLOWER GARDEN: *A Heritage of Blooms*   3

HEARTHSTONES OF HAPPINESS: *Century-Old Cottages and Mansions*   15

HIGHWAYS OF YESTERDAY: *From Indian Trail to Sky Lane*   28

A BOUT WITH DAME FASHION: *A Legislative Anti-Lacing Crusade*   44

HOT STOVE LEAGUES: *Brain Trusters of Yesterday*   51

THE POOR MAN'S CLUB: *Free Lunches and Nickel Beers*   63

A NEW CONFECTION: *Birth of the Ice Cream Sundae*   77

AN OUTMODED INDUSTRY: *A Half Century of Ice Harvesting*   81

THEY KNEW "OLD ABE": *Wisconsin's Civil War Eagle*   86

SORGHUM AND BUCKWHEAT CAKES: *Culinary Favorites of Pioneer Days*   93

CHRISTMAS IN WISCONSIN: *Yuletide Customs Old and New*   105

INDEX   117

SIDE ROADS

Excursions into Wisconsin's Past

Grandmother's Flower Garden:
A Heritage of Blooms

EARLY WISCONSIN WAS IN SUMMER AND FALL A WONDERLAND OF billowing prairie grasses, flowers waltzing in the breeze, and limitless stretches of virgin forest. The Turk's-cap lily vied with the blue of the spiderwort to entrance the eye, and autumn roadsides were splashed with the yellow and purple of countless goldenrods, sunflowers, and asters. Indeed it was as if nature had bidden its representative families of plant life to a central meeting place to display their finery.

This great diversity of plant life may be attributed to the wide range of habitats which Wisconsin provides. Within its borders are woodlands and prairies, bogs and sand lands, rivers and lakes and rocky bluffs. The indigenous plants of the state came into it at different times and from many places. A few may have lived here before the Ice Age. Many northern plants certainly were left here after the retreat of the ice masses. A surprising number of strand plants from the Atlantic coast migrated a thousand miles inland along the sandy shores of the water bodies that were the predecessors of Lake Michigan. Many other species came in from the South and Southeast. Some of our most beautiful flowers have migrated from the Great Plains.

dutchman's breeches

The magnificent display of multicolored flowers and their intricate forms brought cheer to the isolated cabins of the pioneer settlers. From the abundance that nature offered her the early housewife picked and replanted those that most pleased her fancy. May Day was the signal for rural school children to gather flowers on the hillsides and in the valleys—Dutchman's-breeches, rue anemone, trillium, hepatica, pasqueflower, blood-root—and hang them stealthily in decorated homemade paper baskets on the doorknobs of neighboring homes. The aged and the sick were especially remembered.

Until the turn of the century, when a large selection of native flowers was still to be had for the picking, women and children searched the fields and marshes before Decoration (now Memorial) Day for flowers and ferns with which to adorn the graves of their loved ones and the community's soldier dead.

And who among the older folk does not remember the hawthorn and the heavily scented blossoms of the wild crabapple growing on the slopes above the creek bottoms, and again feel the breath of yesterday's springtime?

Much of this splendor has disappeared with the inexorable advance of settlement, but the state still offers displays of flora that are worth almost any effort to see. The largest beds of wild flowers and the greatest number of varieties are to be seen in Door County, the finger of land that points into Lake Michigan.

Northeast of Baileys Harbor and skirted by Moonlight Bay is a series of sand ridges, built up by Lake Michigan's predecessors, where nature planted its choicest flowers. In this region, states Albert M. Fuller, botanist of the Milwaukee Public Museum, grow thirty of Wisconsin's forty-five kinds of native orchids. Here abounds the arctic primrose, rare and extremely local in Wisconsin, and the fringed gentian has found a permanent abode. Here grow all but two of the conifers of Wisconsin. Here, in a scenic spot that for sheer beauty rivals the coast of Maine, is a natural museum, a natural botanical garden, and a natural arboretum. As Mr. Fuller says, "Some cities in the nation would spend millions of dollars to reproduce artificially what nature has formed at Baileys Harbor."

When a movement for more tourist parking facilities threatened Door County's ridges, the public was aroused and local groups took steps to insure the preservation of these wild-flower habitats. The movement was endorsed by Jens Jensen, famous creator of natural landscapes in Chicago's parks, a resident of Door County; the Garden Club of America contributed twelve hundred dollars; and a corporation named The Ridges Sanctuary was formed. "There are generations of Americans on the march," shouted Jens Jensen. "They will be happy for our efforts. Let us not fail them!" Nor did they fail. The ridges of Door County with all their flowers and trees of yesterday were saved for posterity.

At Turville's Point on Lake Monona opposite Madison is another natural grove, where with the first awakening of earth in the spring appear in luxuriant profusion the pasqueflower, the wood anemone, jack-in-the-pulpit, bloodroot, Dutchman's-breeches, wild ginger, and dogtooth violet. On spring and summer evenings the dome of the State Capitol on the farther shore

dwarf
dogwood

is mirrored on the lake. Here it was that Dr. Henry Turville, having relinquished his medical practice, devoted himself to his old-fashioned flower garden. Though he has been dead for a quarter of a century, his neighbors along the shore still miss the morning picture of Dr. Turville, his white hair tossed by the wind, rowing across the lake in his flower boat.

Wild-flower and fern gardens had been described to me a thousand times, but not until I saw them with my own eyes did I have any real conception of their beauty. At Rhinelander, Mosinee, Rockbridge, and elsewhere throughout northern Wisconsin, and in the dry woods south to Wisconsin Dells, grows the trailing arbutus, one of the earliest and most fragrant of all the wild flowers. Before 1929, when the state finally gave legal protection to this charming flower, car lots of the plant were shipped to the markets of Chicago, New York, and other large cities.

trillium

The large-flowered trillium, once common in Wisconsin, was the crowning glory of our May woodlands in days gone by. Today, as a result of unbridled flower-picking and widespread grazing of woodlands, it is nearly extinct in the state. Only a half century ago trillium-picking outings were considered a legitimate diversion, and not until 1929 was this plant protected by law.

On the hillsides of Crawford County, north of Prairie du Chien, the jack-in-the-pulpit thrives in such density that, to quote one landowner, "wagonloads could be removed before they would be even thinned out." South of Wisconsin Rapids large beds of the striking blue lupine, which once flourished on the sandy areas of southern, central, and western Wisconsin, are still an annual attraction for tourists. In the little old cemeteries about Platteville and Dodgeville the shooting star decorates lavishly the graves of the forgotten dead and the untenanted spaces between.

In the sloughs and pools along the Mississippi north to La Crosse grows an abundance of the American lotus, the most publicized of all our wild flowers. Colonies of this plant sometimes cover acres, as do those at Horseshoe Lake near Prairie du Chien and at Black Hawk Slough at De Soto, which have attracted visitors from many places. Throughout the entire state many species of asters and goldenrods contribute their purples and golds to the wealth of color along the autumn roadsides.

The flower without a peer, in the estimation of the European settlers especially, was the water lily, which spread its glorious snow-white blooms, three or four inches in diameter, over the surface of ponds and lakes. "Queen of the inland waters," John Muir called it, "the most beautiful, sumptuous, and deliciously fragrant of all our Wisconsin flowers." In his *Story of My Boyhood and Youth* he relates how he and his companions used to drift among the lilies for hours, and then on the way home gather armfuls of them, which they kept fresh for a week.

Next to the water lily, says Muir, the flower most admired by the early settlers was the pasqueflower, named for the Passover, or Easter, season. It is still the best-loved of the early spring flowers of southern and western Wisconsin. Its appearance in late March or early April has always been regarded as the herald of spring. Muir observes that it is the very first to come out, "covering the cold gray-black ground with cheery blossoms. Before the axe or plough had touched the 'oak openings' of Wisconsin, they were swept by running fires almost every autumn after the grass became dry. If from any cause, such as early snowstorms or late rains, they happened to escape the autumn fire besom, they were likely to be burned in the spring after the

shooting star

snow melted. But whether burned in the spring or fall, ashes and bits of charred twigs and grass stems made the whole country look dismal. Then, before a single grass-blade had sprouted, a hopeful multitude of large hairy, silky buds about as thick as one's thumb came to light, pushing up through the black and gray ashes and cinders, and before these buds were fairly free from the ground they opened wide and displayed purple blossoms about two inches in diameter, giving beauty for ashes in glorious abundance. Instead of remaining in the ground waiting for warm weather and companions, this admirable plant seemed to be in haste to rise and cheer the desolate landscape."

hepatica

About fifty species of ferns grow in Wisconsin. Especially rich in ferns are Rocky Arbor Roadside Park, the Wisconsin Dells area, Devil's Lake State Park, Wyalusing State Park, and Interstate Park. Oddest of them all is the walking fern, which in effect walks over the ground by arching its long, slender fronds until the tips touch the soil and then take root. It is common on moist, shady, mossy limestone ledges in the southern and western parts of the state.

If you have never visited a tamarack bog in early morning, you have missed some of the amazing lessons of plant and insect life. Weird calls of excited birds eager to feed their young beguile you, the soft music of insects fills the air above the stagnant waters, and the sparkling dew sends iridescent flashes of light from pitcher plant, moccasin flower, red osier dogwood, bog rosemary, Canada mayflower, sensitive fern, arrowhead, and swamp birch.

Most of the peat-bog lands of southern Wisconsin have long since been drained for cultivation. One of the few that remain is Hope Lake Bog, two miles north of Cambridge, which still retains its pristine beauty. It was there I had pointed out to me the northern plants that had been left behind after the main retreat of the glacier at the close of the Ice Age. It was there I learned more about the pitcher plant, said to be nourished in part by the dead bodies of the insects that are trapped and drowned in the water basins formed by its pitcher-shaped leaves. Thus the pitcher plant serves as the spider of the plant kingdom. Growing in a circle around the plant root, above which stands a solitary, nodding madder-purple flower, the leaves of the pitcher plant form a chalice which catches the raindrops. The fine hairs that extend downward into the trumpet-shaped leaf permit the easy entrance of bugs and insects but, like the spider's web, make exit impossible. Some botanists believe that the drowned insects also furnish food for the larvae of a fly that later aids in the cross-pollination of the flowers.

For sheer delicacy the pink moccasin flower, also found in the Hope Bog, has few rivals. Beside the heavy-leaved pitcher plant it looks like a lady of refinement and good breeding. The moccasin flower is common toward the north and extends south in pine woods to the Dells of the Wisconsin and to tamarack bogs in the southeastern part of the state.

Peat bogs and wet sphagnous places, which have almost disappeared in southeastern Wisconsin with the growing demand for farm acreage, are still common in the north and as far south as the Wisconsin Dells. There the tamarack bog performs the function that flower preserves do elsewhere. The difficulty of reaching them results in their isolation and permits the propagation of plants that might otherwise be exterminated by grazing cattle or by the burning over of lands to eliminate grass and brush.

One glorious June morning I started for the Wisconsin River, having learned that the plants were blooming on Cactus Bluff *snakewort*

near Sauk City and southward along the river. Meadow larks trilled a welcome from atop the cedar posts along the highway. The course of the river was still hazy, and the grass was wet with dew. Cactus Bluff was ablaze with big yellow, waxy blooms. I picked my way cautiously, having recollections of a previous visit when I had handled a plant carelessly and had spent an entire evening in making applications of adhesive tape and using tweezers to withdraw the minute cactus spines from my tormented flesh.

At length I sat down in utter idleness to view the lovely scene before me and to meditate. From the heights I looked upon a miracle of sky and verdure and inland waterway that must have enchanted the pathfinders as they paddled the Wisconsin River. The very atmosphere seemed haunted by the spirit of a long and mysterious past. I lingered for some time, speculating on how little man knows of God's purpose in creating these rocky bluffs, their brows furrowed by the ages, their feet draped with a festoon of gay flowers quite as beautiful as the lily of the field that neither works nor spins.

On various visits to the region I found the flat-stemmed cactus (*Opuntia Rafinesquii*) at different haunts along the river from Sauk City to Woodman, north to Lake Puckaway and the village of Marquette, and south to New Glarus. The so-called brittle cactus (*Opuntia fragilis*), which grows as far north as St. Croix Falls, is scattered across central Wisconsin and may be correlated with the old buffalo trails. "The brittle cactus," one dairyman of Adams County observed, "is a menace to farmers. It is picked up by the feet of the cattle and causes plenty of trouble. The spines are so sharp that they pierce the leather of heavy army boots."

Of the hundreds of wild flowers known to the pioneers all except one are still residents of Wisconsin. That one is the prairie bush clover, a rare plant which has been collected at only a few points in the state. The last known station was on Barnes Prairie in the central part of Racine County, where Dr. J. J. Davis, for forty years a Racine physician and amateur botanist, collected it in 1880.

Best known of all the wild flowers today is the stemless blue violet. In 1909 this flower was chosen as the state flower by the school children of Wisconsin, receiving almost half of the 147,918 votes that were cast for a variety of flowers, including the wild rose, the trailing arbutus, and the white water lily.

Probably the most accessible habitats of many of the wild flowers, especially the prairie species, are the lands bordering the railway tracks. Protected from the plow, from grazing animals, and from the eyes of thoughtless flower-pickers, they have survived here long after they have been exterminated elsewhere. There is scarcely a community in Wisconsin, moreover, in which some enthusiast does not maintain a wild-flower plot, exacting as this hobby is. The cultivation of wild flowers entails the utmost care and attention, for unless the water, light, and soil requirements of the plant are fully met, it will languish and die.

birdsfoot violet

Among the early horticulturists of Wisconsin two became widely recognized for their flower gardens: Eben E. Rexford of Shiocton and William Toole, Sr. of Baraboo. Rexford is now more famous as the author of the song *Silver Threads among the Gold*, but Toole is still remembered as the "Pansy King" of Wisconsin. On the family's "Garry nee Dule" acres on the outskirts of Baraboo two generations of the Tooles have been most successful in growing and marketing a wide variety of wild flowers. Stately queen of the garden is the black-eyed Susan, which marches across the country in midsummer as herald of the brilliant pageant that is to follow. In this garden the flaming pleurisy root (butterfly weed) rivals many a floral aristocrat with centuries of breeding. Here too will be found the demure asters, blue and purple, assuming the cultivated ways of civilization.

Besides the wild flowers, our grandmothers loved some of the domesticated species: the red, white and pink peony (which they pronounced "piney"), the blue bachelor's-button, sweet william, hollyhock, golden glow, ribbon grass, and yellow rose. Rosendale, in Fond du Lac County, is today recognized as the state's peony town. At the entrance of many cities and villages of Wisconsin are showy displays of hollyhocks, some of which have been grown from seed harvested in the old-fashioned flower garden of the late Dr. Stephen Moulton Babcock, famous inventor of the milk test that has contributed so much to Wisconsin's development as a dairy state. And the Platteville region is known for its culture of the yellow rose.

It was not until the 1870's, when the gradual disappearance of Wisconsin's wild flowers was becoming apparent to many, that the first proposals for their preservation were made, and it was to be another fifty years before protective legislation was passed. In 1923, as a result of the wholesale picking of the "pods" of the American lotus for use in winter bouquets, a law was passed to put a stop to such exploitation of the public lands. Subsequent legislation makes it illegal to pick or dig on public lands, or on private property without the written consent of the owner, the trailing arbutus, all the orchids and trilliums, the wood and the Turk's-cap lily, the pitcher plant, and the shrubby bittersweet.

But laws alone are not enough. As Mr. Fuller has said, "legal protection to be effective must be coordinated with Nature Reserves and education in wild-flower appreciation." Accepting that principle, the Board of Regents of the University of Wisconsin, under the inspiring leadership of Michael B. Olbrich of Madison, established some fifteen years ago an arboretum and wild-life preserve on the shores of Lake Wingra at Madison. This reserve, occupying an area of more than a thousand acres, offers a combination of water, swamp, hill, and prairie. Virtually every variety of soil from peat to clay, sand, and gravel is present, awaiting more extended experimentation to determine what methods of replanting will produce the best results. The pine forest started in 1936 is such an experimentation area. Prairie openings will be given to the planting of oaks. Other plots are being used to test all the other trees that have been common in Wisconsin, from the jack pine of the north to the maples of the south. Actual reforestation work is well advanced.

Nor are the wild flowers and other herbaceous plants neglected. Many species of flowers, especially those of the prairie, have been transplanted to the reservation. Scores of different wild grasses have been moved from swamp and prairie habitats. Dr. John T. Curtis, the University botanist who is supervising the project, envisions it as one of the most useful laboratories of its kind in the world. Once it has been determined under what conditions trees and wild flowers thrive best, the work will be transferred to the roadsides and fields of the state.

In 1941 the Faville Prairie Preserve was established and placed at the disposal of the University for botanical instruction and research in the methods of wild-flower preservation and management. This sanctuary, named for Stoughton W. Faville, a pioneer conservationist, embraces sixty acres near Faville Grove on the west bank of the Crawfish River, between Lake Mills and Waterloo. Here are found numerous species of shrubs, grasses, and flow-

trout lily

ers, including orchids and gentians which once abounded on the prairies of southern Wisconsin but which are now uncommon if not actually rare. It is hoped to develop the reservation into an educational exhibit of all the prairie flora that once covered the southern part of the state.

Dr. Theodore Sperry of the National Park Service expects great benefits to stem from the Faville Prairie Preserve and the University Arboretum at Madison. Whereas we now have in Wisconsin "long strips of land where drought conditions prevail and only unsightly weeds and grasses grow," he says, "some day—if we're lucky—we'll be traveling down colorfully lined, ever-changing highways, seeing somewhat the same countryside that the pioneers of a century ago saw." Thus we may hope that Wisconsin will one day be restored to the native beauty that met the eyes of the pathfinders. Then will grandmother's flower garden bloom again.

lotus

Hearthstones of Happiness: Century-Old Cottages and Mansions

AMONG THE PIONEER HOUSES OF WISCONSIN, ESPECIALLY IN THE smaller cities and villages of the state, are many of marked architectural beauty. Intimately associated with them are the ancestral histories of their builders, for these earlier styles were patterned after the homes in the communities from which the settlers had come. The early architecture of Wisconsin stemmed from that of New England, the Southern states, and the continental countries of Europe and reveals its origin quite as clearly as did the manners and customs of the builders themselves.

In 1934 the federal government sponsored, as a project of the Works Progress Administration, an Historic American Buildings Survey, and appointed Alexander C. Guth of Milwaukee to direct the study for Wisconsin. For a quarter of a century Mr.

Guth's hobby had been architectural history; now, with a staff which at times exceeded twenty-five workers, his work was systematized. Photographs were taken, detailed blueprints made of some fifty-five or sixty buildings, and a brief history compiled of a number of them. So complete are the data assembled that they could be used as working plans for reproducing the structures. All this information has been filed with the Library of Congress in Washington, and a copy of most of it with the State Historical Society in Madison.

One look at the photographs of those buildings in the Society's library was all I needed to start me on another tour of Wisconsin. A know-your-state hobby has become with me almost an obsession. In earlier years I had visited the state's beauty spots, the scenes connected with its unheralded heroes of war and its pioneers of industry, and the communities where people of foreign ancestry have perpetuated the manners and customs of the Old World. Now at long last I had the opportunity to enter the homes of some of the pioneers, sit by their hearthstones, and learn more about the life they had lived.

I was not able to visit all the buildings selected for the Wisconsin old homes exhibit. But once I had learned something of the various architectural types, every house along the roadside took on a new meaning. It is not age alone that makes an old building noteworthy. It must also have an interesting history or some singularity of design or detail.

Several of the houses in which French pioneers lived have become historic. The oldest of Wisconsin dwellings still standing is the cottage built at Green Bay in 1776 by Joseph Roi, a voyageur in the fur trade. With its board-covered walls and partitions of wattle work, it represents the period of transition from log to frame construction. Now called the Porlier-Tank cottage

for two of its later owners, it is maintained as a museum in one of Green Bay's parks.

Up the Fox River at Kaukauna stands the Grignon house, built in 1838 by a grandson of Charles de Langlade, half-breed trapper, trader, and soldier. For this dwelling the materials and workmen were brought by lake boat from Buffalo to Green Bay and thence taken up the river by canoe. Its beautifully carved stair newel, balusters, and handrail rival those in the best contemporary houses in New York. Its acres comprise the oldest homestead in the state that has been in the continuous ownership of a single family.

Another Frenchman's home is the Michael Brisbois residence at Prairie du Chien, probably built shortly after 1840 and reputed to be the oldest stone house in the state. It was plastered inside with lime made from clamshells, and the same substance was used in the mortar that binds the stone walls. The structure has been little altered throughout the decades.

Better known at Prairie du Chien, however, is the extravagant Villa Louis of Hercules L. Dousman, who became Wisconsin's first millionaire. Dousman was the local agent of John Jacob Astor, famous head of the American Fur Company. His House on the Mound, as he called his home, was originally built in 1843 and was extensively remodeled by his widow in 1872. Its beautiful situation overlooking a sweep of the Mississippi River and its spacious rooms, servants' quarters, and handsome antique furniture make it a mecca for tourists. The glories of the fur trade are associated with this building and with other venerable cottages and mansions throughout the state. Every doorway and every stone of them are pages in the history of Wisconsin.

In the main the pioneer houses were built in the colonial tradition. Many of the Southerners who came up the Mississippi to settle in southwestern Wisconsin had ancestral roots in the Atlantic seaboard. Some brought their slaves along. In Platteville, Lancaster, Mineral Point, and neighboring towns are buildings which strongly resemble the homes that were common in Virginia and Kentucky. Among them is the Mitchell-Rountree "stone cottage" in Platteville, which might have been transplanted from the region of the lower James River.

This historic house was built in 1837 by the Reverend Samuel Mitchell and has sheltered five generations of Mitchells and Rountrees. Mitchell, a Virginian, had served in the American Revolution and was with Washington's troops at Yorktown when Cornwallis surrendered. A covered walk formerly connected the house with a kitchen in the rear yard, whence colored servants carried piping-hot food to the dining room. Like most Southern homes of the period, it has both a parlor and a sitting room; a hall runs the length of the building; chair rails extend around the walls. On the mahogany sideboard there was a real touch of the Old South: jars filled with rose petals. "This is one of the most charming houses found in the entire Wisconsin survey," wrote Mr. Guth in his final report.

Nearby stands the residence of the Kentucky-born Major John H. Rountree, "father of Platteville," who in 1828 had married Mary Grace Mitchell, daughter of Samuel Mitchell, then a pastor in Galena. This house was restored in 1945 to serve as the home of the president of Platteville State Teachers College. Originally built in 1854, it is set high above the valley, through which runs a picturesque little stream. The long two-story, red-brick building, with its five white pillars and double porch across the front, is reminiscent of Southern colonial days. The sloping lawn is dotted with ancient oaks and elms. Little of the Rountree furniture remains. The large table at which General U. S.

Grant ate while he was a guest of the family is now in the rooms of the local Masonic lodge.

Much could be written about Platteville homes. Every old building was an invitation to me to explore further. Every door-step beckoned. But this was not to be a detailed study of domestic architecture. I was touring the state to find the homes and surroundings that produced so many men and women of real purpose. Whence came that strength of character among the pioneers, that sturdiness that partook of the oaks and hickories in their fields?

A side road led me to the territorial capitol at Belmont. What a thrill one feels as he stands in those halls where in 1836 men dreamed of the greatness of the Wisconsin that was to be! This first capitol was merely a temporary frame structure which had  the square false front that was common to many of the store-residences of the period. There was a moving simplicity about it all, and I found myself thinking of such men as James Duane Doty, capital-site promoter, Henry Dodge, rugged territorial governor, and Charles Dunn, first chief justice of Wisconsin.

territorial capitol

I now turned toward Mineral Point, where a group of Cornish miners settled in the early days of the territory. Mineral Point has always reminded me of Fredericksburg, Virginia; both have kept their youth. If you can visit only a single Old World community of Wisconsin's territorial era, then by all means go to Mineral Point, which probably offers the best opportunity to study the pioneer architecture of the state. Plan to stay at least an entire day; a week would be better. The low dwellings of the Cornish settlers, of soft-brown native stone, were built right into the hillsides, which were skirted by narrow streets below. Each of the houses is surmounted by three to five chimneys, arising from the fireplaces which are niched into every available corner;

the windows are deeply recessed, the doors six-paneled. "These houses and their surroundings," says John F. Kienitz, professor of art history in the University of Wisconsin, "help us to understand the cultural backgrounds of Wisconsin. We have here a direct continuation of the medieval stone craftsmanship of England. It is no accident that makes these Cornish dwellings so attractive to the eye. They were built from the heart."

Besides these stone houses of the Cornish miners, there still stand in Mineral Point some of the log houses of other early settlers, two-storied buildings that reflect the glory of the deep South and cottages erected by the Welsh, whose pocket settlements mingle with those of Cousin Jack.

octagon house
Watertown

Still in use in Wisconsin are some of the octagonal and hexagonal houses of a bygone era. These architectural oddities can be seen in a dozen cities from Lancaster to Hudson, from Milwaukee to Green Bay. Their ancestor is the hexagonal Goodrich house at Milton, built in 1844. This house made a strong appeal to one Orson Squire Fowler of New York, a queer character who wrote popular books on sex, temperance, and tight lacing and amassed a fortune preaching phrenology. After seeing the Goodrich dwelling on one of his many lecture tours in Wisconsin, he designed and erected a more pretentious one high up on the bank of the Hudson. He then wrote a book advocating this style of architecture as the most healthful and inspirational for the occupants. With the distribution of *A Home for All* in the late forties was inaugurated a building fad among the elite which is exemplified in numerous houses still standing in Wisconsin: at Elkhorn, Fond du Lac, Prairie du Chien, Whitewater, Horicon, Pewaukee, Fort Atkinson, Neenah, and elsewhere.

Among them is the Richards house at Watertown, a four-story stone structure crowning a hill. It was equipped with hot-

and cold-air ducts and was thus probably the first building in the West to be air-conditioned. The Watertown Historical Society, the present occupant, states that it was this house which furnished the inspiration for the "House of Tomorrow" at the Century of Progress Exposition held in Chicago in the mid-thirties.

Architects were few in the early days, and thus every builder and craftsman was free to incorporate into the structures he built his own ideas of comfort and beauty. The result was a wide variety of home architecture in Wisconsin. At Racine the old Hunt House, built in 1842, is considered a fine example of the Greek revival period; near Portage is the Old Agency House, built in 1832, which architects cite as an essentially New England frame dwelling constructed on larger proportions; at Prospect Hill in Waukesha County is the Vanderpool farm home, another dwelling of colonial design, with antiquated summer kitchen and woodshed attached.

Along the way I saw many other novel and attractive homes. At Beloit, for example, I saw the three houses built of cobblestones, pointed with such precision as to appear the work of a jeweler rather than a mason; near Mukwonago the eighty-year-old farm home of Everett Martin, constructed of fieldstone; at the White River crossing near Burlington the sandstone houses built by the Mormons; and southeast of Kirchhayn the picturesque Christian Turck log house with its overhanging wooden sunshade. Throughout the northern part of the state I often peeped through trees at the mammoth frame palaces of the region's lumbermen, reminiscent of the houses owned by men of wealth along the Massachusetts seashore at Marblehead.

Scattered throughout southern Wisconsin are numerous plain little farmhouses. Some have an upright of two stories with an

"ell" or lean-to. Others slope away at the back, the extension being used for kitchen, pantries, storeroom, and woodshed. Historically these are the English farmhouses of an early era, the seventeenth and eighteenth centuries especially. The long slope of the roof over the lean-to side of the house is called in England a catslide. Locally both types of structure are known as "Yankee houses." Built in accordance with plans derived from carpenter's manuals of the day, they are the most common of the many old houses still standing. It is a pity that stone so soon became too costly to use for construction, for stone mellows more with age than wood and withstands the years with less decay. Frame structures often need to be banked in winter with cornstalks, marsh hay, or horse manure.

Many of the pioneers who came from the Old World, when faced with the difficulties of founding a home in unsettled Wisconsin, designed architectural styles of their own. Thus the Norwegians constructed houses of logs covered with a roof made of earth, replicas of which may be seen in the "Little Norway" community near Mount Horeb. In Door County after the Peshtigo fire of 1873 the Belgians replaced their log homes with dwellings of red brick made from their own soil. Their villages remind one of the pictures in the story books of their native land. The Finns who colonized on the cutover lands between Superior and Ashland mortised logs and fitted them together with a cabinetmaker's precision. Of all the very early houses these were probably the warmest.

Often the foreign-born settler placed in his yard some symbol of his native land that added a touch of Old World picturesqueness to the domestic scene: a Dutch windmill, a German smokehouse, a crucifix beside the family entrance, rows of Bavarian beehives. The Yankee had a woodshed.

Norwegian springhouse

That old woodshed, sometimes attached to the house and sometimes a separate structure a little distance away, called up far more memories than did the house itself. Here were kept the switches that were used to administer punishment to naughty children. Here the cooking was done in summer and fall. Behind the stove stood baskets of chips with which the fires were started; on the wall hung great hams encased in bags; and from the ceiling hung the drying seed corn. Near the stove stood a rocking chair, so faced that the vigilant occupant might superintend the cooking and at the same time watch that mischievous chickens did not invade the vegetable garden.

The shed was likewise a storehouse. Pushed out of the way until Saturday night, when there would be family baths, was a washtub. Neat piles of sawed pine and maple, oak and hickory, titillated the nostrils with their rich aroma. Over in a corner or above the stove were odds and ends of wire, an old bootjack, or a surcingle of sleighbells. All was shipshape. The fellow with a woodshed could find what he needed when he needed it. Near the doorway, topping the clothes post, hung pail and dinner bell. "When traveling and hungry, stop at a home where there is a dinner bell," admonished the late Solomon Levitan, pack peddler, philosopher, and for six terms state treasurer of Wisconsin. "These people always have plenty of food to put on the table."

In winter the woodshed was the place where you took off your wooden shoes or overshoes, a temporary storehouse for all cast-off garments, and a shelter and workroom for the chopping block and sawbuck. Civilization was cruel when it deprived us of the old woodshed.

Doorways! May I never forget them! Nowhere in the world, perhaps, are there any passways so historic, so inhabited by the

me, portraits of human beings who had been a part of the pioneer saga. Their very names carried an aroma of the past, for their elders had had different ideas about naming their children than does the present-day parent. Often it was a family mood or a Christian virtue that supplied the name: Thankful, Patience, Final, Elementary, Pleasy, Remember, Hope, Faith, Charity, Joy, Silence. As a compromise with their pastors, who usually preferred to honor the saints, parents added a second name, such as George, Joseph, John, William, Fred, Paul, Peter, Henry, Patrick, Ann, Abigail, Margaret, Mary, Martha, Elizabeth, Catherine. Of the nicknames bestowed upon the child after he started to school the census reports contain no record.

For the whole family a kind of aura hung over the old homestead. As the sons grew to maturity, they were told not only the house but even the room of their birth. The mother and even the neighbor woman who had acted as midwife cherished the hope that the event would one day prove to be memorable, that the house might become a mecca like the birthplaces of Washington, Webster, Lincoln, and other American heroes. No such hope can be entertained for their great-grandchildren, ninety per cent of whom are born in hospitals under the ministrations of a doctor.

In most homes of that era before the turn of the century there was an upright organ. Around it on winter evenings gathered the young folk of the family and neighboring households to sing the songs of the day: *When You and I Were Young, Maggie; After the Ball;* and *Daisy Belle.* Father, in his stocking feet, sat comfortably in the kitchen, smoking his pipe or drowsing by the stove; Mother sat in a rocking chair knitting. A little later all of them would join in popping corn or pulling molasses candy. None of them had ever heard of a vamp, a permanent, a cafeteria, a chain store, or a roadhouse. Gingham could be purchased for five cents a yard. A girl's waist had to be tapered and small enough to be encircled by two hands. By half past nine the party was over, all lights were out, and the countryside lay wrapped in the stillness of a rural night.

As our family drove through the villages and cities of our region in my boyhood days, we looked at the hitching posts before people's houses. For that was the yardstick of wealth. A cedar post told us that the occupants of the house were in poor or modest circumstances; a post topped with a steel ornament, that they were comfortably well-to-do; some such contraption as a cast-iron dog or metal statue of a Negro boy holding the tie-ring, that the family was "rich." It was an easy way to evaluate the financial status of the districts through which we passed.

The first settlers loved their homes and their acres. Now, some generations later, many of these old farms and village residences are tenanted by other families. But somehow the name of the pioneer builder and tiller of the soil still clings to the house. The new owner may not even sense the reason. But the community remembers. The State Historical Society, in cooperation with the University's College of Agriculture, has compiled records which reveal that some 265 farmsteads of the state have been in the same family for at least a century, and some longer. These cottages and mansions are monuments to the character of their occupants and the era that produced them. From the scroll of such men and their achievements, history is written. The world owes to the pioneer a debt it must never forget.

Highways of Yesterday: From Indian Trail to Sky Lane

MOST OF US DO NOT EASILY ENVISAGE A LIMITLESS WILDERNESS UNbroken by civilization's roads and highways. But such a region was all of Wisconsin three hundred years ago when the white man first set foot upon it—mile after mile of deep forest alternating with open prairie, threaded by the innumerable streams and creeks that served as the first lanes of travel. In such a land the wayfarer was dependent on nature's landmarks to guide him on his course.

In southern Wisconsin, a few miles from the Wisconsin River, is an eminence shrouded in a soft veil of azure mists which is fittingly called Blue Mounds. Rising to a height of some twelve hundred feet above Lake Michigan, it is the loftiest point in southern Wisconsin and served both the Indian and the early white man as a landmark and lookout post. From its topmost crest one may today look down upon seven counties of the state. Truly magnificent are the views that meet the eye: to the south a panorama of rolling prairies, pricked by the spires of country churches; to the east the dome of the Capitol at Madison, twenty-five miles away; to the north and west bold headlands mantled with trees, through which break occasional flashes of silver, mapping the sinuous course of the Wisconsin River.

Blue Mounds was undoubtedly one of the earliest guideposts for both red and white man in Wisconsin. Legend has it that hither the Indians trekked from time immemorial, confident that a draught of the sparkling waters gushing from its side would insure a safe journey to the Happy Hunting Ground. On the north slope still stand some of the "trail trees" that once pointed the easier way to the spring—or perhaps to the nearby Four Lakes region, or to the Wisconsin River and connecting trails leading through the dark forest to remote Indian villages. Such trail trees, bent in this or that direction while they were still pliant saplings, were the Indian's guideposts.

For the early white man as well as the Indian the lakes and rivers of the region were the first highways. For more than a century and a half after 1673, when the intrepid Marquette and Jolliet made their memorable canoe journey down the Fox and Wisconsin rivers to the Mississippi, the European explorer and fur trader traveled almost exclusively by water. Ultimately the French established a fur-trading post at either end of the Fox-Wisconsin route, at Green Bay and Prairie du Chien, and gradually these developed into the first permanent settlements.

By the early 1820's another area, the lead and zinc region of southwestern Wisconsin, had become a mecca for prospectors and settlers. Legally it was a part of the vast domain of Michigan Territory, as was all the country now included in Wisconsin. For a number of years James Duane Doty, in his capacity of district judge, made an annual journey from his home in Green Bay to Prairie du Chien. His early trips were made in the time-honored manner, in a bark canoe over the Fox-Wisconsin waterway. But in 1829 he abandoned his canoe. In May of that year he and his companions, Morgan L. Martin and Henry S. Baird, completed what is believed to have been the first overland journey made by white men across Wisconsin. Traveling on horseback with a Menominee guide, the party followed the Indian trails that meandered through the lush virgin forests.

As settlements multiplied, this mode of travel became not only more practicable but necessary. The delegates to the first meeting of the Wisconsin territorial legislature, who assembled at Belmont in the autumn of 1836, had traveled on horseback over the Indian trails. They kept their bearings with the help of such natural signposts as Blue Mounds, Belmont Mound, Platte Mound, and Sinsinawa Mound.

In the meantime the building of military roads had begun. After the War of 1812 the Americans had built two forts, Fort Howard at Green Bay and Fort Crawford at Prairie du Chien, both on the sites of earlier French posts. Later, in 1828, Fort Winnebago was established near Portage as the connecting link. At these posts garrisons were maintained to protect fur traders and settlers against Indian attack and depredation. Unofficially the region was called by the name of the river crossing it, a name variously written Ouiscousin, Ouiscouching, Wiskonsan, and Wiskonsin until the spelling was finally fixed by Congress and the territorial legislature.

Because of the difficulty of transporting supplies to the garrisons, especially in winter, Congress was forced to make some provision for the building of roads. After 1832, when the publicity attending the Black Hawk War advertised the fertility of the lands, the region was invaded by a flood of settlers who clamored loudly for roads. In 1830 and 1832, while Wisconsin was still a part of Michigan Territory, Congress appropriated the sum of seven thousand dollars for a road from Fort Howard to Prairie du Chien. The road followed well-trodden Indian trails for a good part of the way and was built by troops from the two forts.

The soldiers began work in 1835, and the next year the road was in operation, although it was far from adequate. It was a highway of the crudest sort, entirely unsurfaced, and usable only in winter when the ground was frozen. In summer it was a mire, despite the fact that it followed the higher ridges wherever possible. The story is told of a Fond du Lac hotelkeeper who once tossed a hat and a pair of shoes into the road morass outside his hostelry in order to induce early morning passers-by to dig for a man who had been drowned on land! Today the route of this Old Military Road can be traced by markers that have been placed along its course, though the road is difficult to tour. The best-known section, probably, is the stretch that joins with the old Wanona trail, a mile-long path between the Wisconsin and Fox rivers over which the voyageurs and trappers of two centuries ago transported their packs. For twenty miles westward out of Mount Horeb the North Western Railroad is built on the bed of the old road.

The rapid increase in population after 1830 forced the building of several other military highways. During the years 1838 and 1839 Congress appropriated money for roads from Green Bay, through Milwaukee, to the southern boundary of the territory; from Milwaukee, through Madison, to Dubuque; from Ra-

cine, through Janesville, to Sinipee on the Mississippi River
(south of present-day Potosi); from Sauk Harbor (Port Washington) on Lake Michigan to Dekorra on the Wisconsin River;
from Fond du Lac, through the town of Fox Lake, to the Wisconsin River.

The old "Post Road" from Green Bay to Milwaukee is one of
the oldest highways in the Middle West. Over it in winter traveled the lonely mail carrier, hustling along night and day to
keep from freezing. In summer the mails were carried by boat.

In the meantime the territorial legislature was also making
provision for road-building. By 1848, when Wisconsin became
a state, almost 250 roads had been authorized, expenses for
which were to be borne by the localities they served or by private parties. But fewer than a third of these roads were actually
built during the territorial period, all but fourteen south of the
Fox and Wisconsin rivers.

At the same time Congress was being entreated to allot lands
for the building of canals. Failing to obtain such federal grants,
the territorial legislature in 1838 chartered the Milwaukee and
Rock River Canal Company. This organization was empowered
to build and maintain a continuous water route between Lake
Michigan and the Mississippi River, where it would connect
with steamboat facilities to the St. Louis and New Orleans markets. The federal government lent some assistance and digging
was started in the Milwaukee River. But the project, already
outmoded by the incipient railroad-building, was never completed except for the short canal connecting the Fox and Wisconsin rivers at Portage. This canal was finished in 1851 and is
still in use, but it has been only a partial success. No engineering
skill has been able to keep it open for the deep-draught vessels
of the present day.

In their frenzy to get lead, wheat, and pork to market, the settlers of the forties and fifties also demanded plank roads, an Old Country innovation. Before 1871 charters were granted to 135 road-building companies. The most successful of their projects was the Milwaukee-Watertown Plank Road, constructed in 1847, which was soon yielding revenues up to thirteen hundred dollars a week. But the system was soon outmoded, and in 1869 the legislators authorized town supervisors to convert into a public highway any road that had been out of repair for sixty days.

It was during this period of the plank road that the stagecoach reached its height. Stagecoach owners made contracts with the federal government for carrying the mail, and to supplement their revenues they carried passengers as well. The stage drivers were a rough, daring, and prankful set of frontiersmen. Among them was "Jerry" Rusk, later governor of the state and a member of the president's cabinet. When Jerry dropped his reins to enter the Union Army he became the hero of the stage-driving fraternity.

As the stagecoach system reached out into all sections of the state, hotels and inns sprang up along their routes. The best of them offered the guest a room furnished with homemade bedsteads, straw or cornhusk ticks, heavy bedding, and a top quilt of stagecoach-wheel design or, if the weather was cold, a buffalo robe. These inns became one of the institutions of the period. They served good food, including game and strong drink, and were the scenes of many a convivial gathering. Snatches of the lusty songs that were sung and the ribald jokes that were told still survive in the folklore of the West.

A few of the hostelries themselves have lingered on into the present generation: the Robert Dunkel Inn halfway between

Milwaukee and Waukesha, the Okauchee House at Okauchee, the cobblestone Jesse Smith Inn southwest of Big Bend, the Ruggles Inn near Ridgeway, the Wade House in Greenbush, west of Sheboygan Falls, Mag Lawe, north of Shawano, the Dodgeville Hotel, and numerous others.

Any mention of the hardships of travel in those Civil War days of rough corduroy roads and bridges brings to my mind the chuckles with which Doane Robinson, a farmer living south of Castle Rock in Monroe County, would recall "the grumbling and cursing of travelers as the big stage rumbled and bounded over the corduroy logs, the white horses on the keen gallop and the passengers tossed from their seats bumping their heads on the coach roof."

The outbreak of the Civil War again presented a problem of military roads. Early in 1863 Congress, mindful of the danger of military invasion through Canada, appropriated public lands for the building of a military wagon road from Green Bay to Fort Wilkins, in the vicinity of Ontonagon on Lake Superior. This road ultimately became the property of the state. One section of it, which passed through the Menominee Indian Reservation, was popularly known as the Abraham Lincoln Road. A similar military wagon road, authorized by Congress in 1864 but not completed until 1870, extended along the Wisconsin River from Wausau to Gilbert, and thence to Fort Wilkins. These two roads became the principal arteries of the early lumbering industry and the settlement of vast sections of northern Wisconsin.

After Wisconsin became a state in 1848 every session of the legislature authorized the construction of state roads that were to be locally financed. The counties and towns were also empowered to build roads within their confines. These were supported by a toll tax, which the citizen might pay either in money or by doing a specified amount of labor on the roads. Such a system inevitably produced deplorable results. In spring every vehicle became mired. Typical of conditions everywhere was the village of Watertown, where in the middle of the street a sign borne aloft on a tall pole carried the warning "No Bottom." For the convenience of the poor fellow who got stuck, an ox team stood ready to pull him and his wagon out of the mud.

As settlement advanced to areas north of the Fox-Wisconsin route, bridges were erected over many of the streams by private companies, which were permitted to collect tolls from the traffic crossing them. Some of these bridges were boarded over to protect the planking from the elements. Best known to early travelers were the toll bridges at Bridgeport, Boscobel, Muscoda, and the Clarence Crossing near Brodhead. Over such bridges, in the covered wagons of the day, traveled the migrants who settled the West.

In a quiet dale of Ozaukee County, spanning Cedar Creek a few miles north of Cedarburg, is the last of the covered bridges still standing in Wisconsin. It was erected in 1876. I often drive out of my way to listen to the creaks it utters, as if it were again groaning under the weight of the heavy oxen-drawn loads it once bore across the stream. Bent though it is from years of service, it bears the local farmers quite as safely as it did when its last dowels and wedges were driven tight. Grayed from the sun and snows of many decades, it tells a hundred tales to the wayfarer who bends a sympathetic ear. It is a heritage of the past.

The prospect of railway transportation aroused the keenest interest, even in territorial days. The difficulty of getting crops to market was so great that it threatened for a time to produce

covered bridge

an exodus of settlers from western Wisconsin. In the very first
session of the territorial legislature there was agitation for the
building of railroads. Not until fifteen years later did this agitation bear fruit, but in 1851 the Milwaukee and Mississippi
River Railway, predecessor of the Chicago, Milwaukee and St.
Paul, opened a line from Milwaukee to Waukesha, which had
been built with the aid of Eastern capital. In 1854 it was extended to Madison, and three years later to the Mississippi
River. By 1859 another line, forerunner of today's North Western, was in operation from Oshkosh to Janesville, where it made
connections for Chicago. Five years later it offered continuous
service from Chicago to Green Bay, via Janesville, Fond du
Lac, Oshkosh, and Appleton.

These achievements inspired the greatest enthusiasm, and
the arrival of the iron horse at a town or village was the occasion
for a lively celebration. So anxious were the rural areas for better transportation facilities that farmers mortgaged their farms
to help in railway construction. Many ultimately lost them, for
the Panic of 1857 threw every Wisconsin railroad into bank-
ruptcy. Scores of smaller lines, developed through community
enterprise, later consolidated with the larger systems. Most
picturesque of these, perhaps, was the narrow-gauge line from
Woodman to Fennimore. When viewed from a distance as it
curved around the hills of that rugged southwestern country,
it looked like a railroad system in miniature. For half a century,
until about 1900, the railroads continued to occupy first place
in the state's transportation system.

One reform promoted by the railroads has affected every human being in America. Until the 1880's all time throughout the
country was local or "solar" time; when the clock in Madison
said 11:10, it was 11:16 in Milwaukee and 11:17 in Chicago.

But on Sunday, November 18, 1883, "standard" time, sponsored by the railroads, was adopted throughout the United States. Thereafter people went to the railroad station to "get the right time." Before the telephone came into general use I often saw groups of farmers gather at the smaller depots in Wisconsin with big watches in their hands, ready to set them when the time signal came over the telegraph wire. But not until thirty-five years later, on March 19, 1918, did the government officially recognize the standard time zones.

Those years prior to 1900, before the automobile came into general use, are often called the "horse-and-buggy days." In the summertime, if the roads were passable, families went to church in surreys and two-spring phaetons. The steel-rimmed wheels that were used for a time produced a grinding, nerve-needling sound as they made contact with the gravel or stone roadways. If the weather was inclement the horses were stabled when they arrived at the church in the long sheds provided for the purpose. On weekdays the menfolk drove to town in either a democrat or a lumber wagon, the boys often in a buckboard or a two-wheeled cart. Every store in town had its hitching post, where the horses stomped deep holes in the road as they stood fighting the flies. Whenever a group of farmers gathered to chat, they were almost sure to boast chestily that they owned a "Clark" (Oshkosh) or a "Stratman" (Dodgeville) carriage; a "Mitchell-Lewis" (Racine) or a "Mandt" (Stoughton) wagon; a "Streich" (Oshkosh) or an "Anti-tip" (Stoughton) bobsleigh.

"Where were the pungs made?" I asked a professor in the College of Agriculture at the University.

"A pung," he repeated, and hesitated. "That was a kind of sleigh box on straight runners. Something like a toboggan. Every early-day farmer had one. I guess they were homemade." In the late sixties William Van Schaick of North Walworth, Wisconsin, patented the coupling that made it possible to turn sleighs around. It was immediately adopted by all countries using bob-sleds. The original model is in the possession of the Walworth County Historical Society.

In 1900 the state of Wisconsin stood fourth in the nation in the manufacture of carriages and wagons. Of 436 such concerns in the state, about thirteen per cent were in the Wisconsin cities of Milwaukee, Oshkosh, La Crosse, Sheboygan, and Racine. Even then the industry had begun to decline, however, the number of factories being less than it had been a decade earlier. The ominous signs of the future were already apparent to the carriage-wagon industrialists.

Toward the close of the horse-and-buggy days another vehicle, the bicycle, became popular. Old and young peddled along the country roads, the men dressed like many of the golfers of a later day, in knee breeches and long yarn stockings. Usually the riders walked up the hills. Often they carried squirt guns loaded with ammonia to repel chasing dogs. Professional men, the lower extremities of their pants legs snapped in guards to prevent entanglements with the sprocket wheels, bicycled to their offices. Some of the stagecoach inns were temporarily re-vived. At all summer gatherings there were races. Bicyclists who could afford to do so subscribed to the *American Wheel-man* and joined the Wisconsin League for Good Roads. A Mil-waukee man, Otto Dorner, became chairman of a committee of the national organization that was working for better roads. George W. Peck, governor of the state in the early nineties and author of *Peck's Bad Boy,* took a lively interest in the movement. It was not until 1901, however, that a law was passed authoriz-ing counties to build bicycle paths along public roads and streets. It was belated legislation, for interest in the bicycle had already begun to lag. Even then the automobile was in sight.

Some day a novelist will write the story of Wisconsin's early interest in the invention of the automobile. For twenty-five years it was in the hearts and on the minds of its people. Coming as they did from many places and many lands, they wanted contact with their friends, and they deeply resented the condition of the roads which at many seasons made travel impossible. Open fields, hills, and drifting clouds were beckoning, and they could not respond. They wanted to travel the highways faster than the horse and buggy could carry them.

In 1871 Dr. J. W. Carhart of Racine designed and operated the first self-propelled highway vehicle in the United States. It was a two-cylinder steam-engine contraption which made so much noise that the whole populace turned out when it took to the road. "When I went to Paris in 1905 to receive the award and certificate of honor for this invention," Carhart boasted afterward, "the earliest other exhibit at the exposition was invented in 1894—just twenty-three years later than my own."

Carhart's vehicle was not a success, but it offered an idea and inspired many hopes. In 1875 the legislature offered a reward of ten thousand dollars for the invention of a self-propelled vehicle that would make a run of two hundred miles on Wisconsin highways. Two years later the route was designated as the two-hundred-mile stretch from Green Bay to Madison, and judges were appointed to decide the outcome of the contest.

When the day of the contest arrived, only two vehicles were entered, the "Green Bay" and the "Oshkosh." Both were driven by steam power, the one being of horizontal-boiler, and the other of vertical-boiler design. Like the railroad locomotives of the day, both were wood-burners. The race—the first motor-vehicle race in the United States—began on July 16, 1878. All along the route from Green Bay to Madison the populace had turned out to await the arrival of the vehicles. The Green Bay took the lead and kept it until it was within a few miles of Madison, when it broke down. The Oshkosh now steamed ahead and won the race, having covered 201 miles in thirty-three hours and twenty-seven minutes, or an average of about six miles an hour. The legislature, after debating and wrangling over payment of the prize money, finally voted to award five thousand dollars to the owners of the Oshkosh.

The people were not discouraged. Mechanics in all parts of the state kept on tinkering. Milwaukee claims that a car made by one of its residents, a cooper named Gottfried Schloemer, was the first gasoline-run automobile ever operated in the United States. It wouldn't make a hill, and it couldn't back up, since it had no reverse gear. The Schloemer car is preserved in the Milwaukee Public Museum.

A really lively competition now began to develop among inventors. In 1894 A. W. Ballard of Oshkosh built a machine which was chain-driven like a bicycle. When it won a race with a horse around Lake Winnebago, a Wausau physician, Dr. Douglas L. Sauerhering, ordered a Ballard car, which was delivered the next spring. This machine seated four people, who rode back to back on upholstered seats, with a backrest between them. It also had kerosene lamps, so that the doctor could get home when he was caught out after dark. The first automobile to have pneumatic tires is said to have been the machine invented by E. J. Pennington and manufactured by the Racine Hardware Manufacturing Company in 1895. By 1901 a Duryea car was being demonstrated by Lucia Brothers, a sporting-goods firm at Green Bay, as a boon to the traveling man whose business was done with country customers. But in these early days of experimentation "hardly anyone had a good word for the automobile," said Howard E. Lucia twenty years later. "Everyone ridiculed it and predicted that we would break our necks. When we broke down on the roads nobody would help us."

But the automobile had come to stay. In 1905, when there were sixteen hundred cars in the state, registration was begun. The first license was issued to Judge A. G. Zimmerman of Madison, who drove a vehicle with a rear passenger entrance. The registration fee was one dollar and was good for the life of the car. In 1909 the fee was doubled, and after 1911 annual registration was required.

The first registrar, Alexander J. Cobban, had his troubles. The automobile was still a new contrivance, and it was perhaps natural that certain old superstitions should attach to it. Dozens of license plates were returned because the number 13 was mixed up in the combination somewhere. When Emery A. Odell, a publisher of Monroe, actually applied for and received the number 13, his request was deemed worthy of newspaper space. Many applicants were disturbed when they could not obtain a number below 100.

With the arrival of the automobile the small voice of the bicyclists begging for better roads swelled to a vociferous clamor. The Good Roads movement, with the advice and cooperation of W. O. Hotchkiss, state geologist, gained impetus. In 1908, against the protests of the southern counties, which already had good roads, the constitution was amended, by a vote of three to one, to permit the state to engage in the building of roads. Within ten years a highway network of five thousand miles was in the building. More than fifty makes of cars designed, named, and produced in Wisconsin machine shops, garages, and factories were sold before 1930, when big business took over the industry nationally. Only a few names were contributed to present-day cars.

Goggled, scarved, and clad in linen dusters, seated at the right, farm fashion, early autoists started their journeys. Sometimes such a cloud of road dust was stirred up that passing cars had to stop or slow down until the atmosphere had cleared. Drivers preferred to return before dusk, for the early kerosene and the subsequent acetylene lighting systems were temperamental affairs. Farseeing blacksmiths converted their shops into garages and did repair work.

Before 1915 every session of the legislature witnessed a contest between the owners of sleighs and the drivers of automobiles. The farmers wanted the standard width of sleighs to be fixed wide enough so that heavy hauling could be safely done. Automobile owners, on the other hand, urged that sleighs be the same width as motor vehicles in order to lessen the danger of getting stuck in the snow. Better roads and the snowplow finally settled both problems satisfactorily.

Financed by a tax on gasoline, arteries of concrete and asphalt lengthen year after year. What was fixed as the saturation point for automobile ownership in 1910 has been trebled. Overextended railroad and interurban lines and antiquated streetcar systems have had to be discontinued and their tracks removed. Not a bright Sunday passes that half the Wisconsin population is not on wheels, and not a summer that the state is not visited by several million tourists.

These are some of the changes that have taken place since that winter in 1860 when Assemblyman Asaph Whittlesey traveled on snowshoes from his home in Ashland to the Capitol in Madison. Ahead of us are many more changes. Since 1940 many of Whittlesey's successors in the legislature have traveled over the airline routes that now crisscross the state. Blue Mounds, by-passed by a state trunk highway but still wrapped in mists of blue, awaits the day when it will again point the way. On this hill where Indian braves once flashed signals to their confederates in the nearby "hollers" and on the prairies, television towers are to rise that will bring to the people of today's Wisconsin scenes and voices from beyond the horizon's rim.

A Bout with Dame Fashion: A Legislative Anti-Lacing Crusade

ONE OF THE UNMENTIONABLES OF A BYGONE GENERATION'S DAILY life was the woman's corset. Boned, stayed, and tightly laced, it was for many decades an indispensable article of apparel for milady who bowed to fashion's decrees. Men, too, countenanced the fad, but only—asserted the anti-lacing crusaders—because they didn't have to wear them. "Let man try for himself," wrote one of them at the turn of the century, "what it means to spend a day in well-laced corsets, a summer's day preferably, when the blood-vessels respond to the dilating warmth. It would serve him for a liberal education and temper forever his strange masculine and inartistic enthusiasm for wasp-waists. For it would prove to him once and for all time the cost at which the nineteen inches are gained."

44

Wisconsin had its role both in the development of these "instruments of torture" and in their ultimate disappearance from the scene of Vanity Fair. Among the corset designers of the nineteenth century was the now-forgotten Freeman L. Tripp, an inventor and the owner of a women's apparel shop in Eau Claire early in the sixties. In later life he cited as his most noteworthy achievement the hat fastener he had invented to eliminate the need for ribbons tied under the chin. Fifteen years earlier, in 1863, he had patented another article in which, one hopes, he took less pride. This was a corset fashioned with whalebone, which was already in general use as stiffening for the hoop skirt. This invention he sold to a traveling salesman from Chicago for five hundred dollars. A few years later he devised another model, a long-waisted garment which he sold for the same amount. Among his other creations were a low-busted corset emphasizing the wasp waist, which immediately became popular, and an abdominal model that proved to be a money-maker.

Well into the twentieth century women continued to lace themselves tightly into heavily boned garments to achieve the minimum waistline, eighteen or nineteen inches being the goal. Surely none but Dame Fashion could have imposed so rigorous a discipline! "That the stays are indeed tight," protested Dr. Arabella Kenealy in 1904 in the *Nineteenth Century* magazine, "is shown by the fact that although the physique and internal organs expand in every other direction, the waist of adult woman *is actually less than that of the girl between ten and twelve.*"

The wearing of corsets was of course by no means new in history; for centuries it had been fashionable among the leisure classes of Europe. But it was not until the late nineteenth century that the working classes adopted the practice. "At the present moment," Dr. Kenealy wrote despairingly, "the use of corsets is more universal than has hitherto been known.... It permeates the humblest levels of society. You shall not find a housemaid or kitchenmaid, a shop-girl or a little slave of all work, who does not pinch her waist to a morbid and ridiculous extent. The thing has become, indeed, a national evil." Nor did she dare hope that reform could be accomplished within a generation. "Progress is far too slow a thing for that."

But the next generation did see the doom of tight lacing, thanks to the fulminations of the medical profession, the mania for reform which seized the early twentieth century, and the growing emancipation of women on every front. The injuries caused by tight lacing were described in detail by scientists; one of them even performed experiments with corseted monkeys, the results of which were "as disastrous as they were instructive." And Dr. Kenealy was not the only woman to appeal to feminists with the warning that "so long as one sex wantonly curtails its powers and the other one does not, so long will the sex that does be heavily and insuperably handicapped."

At about the same time the anti-lacing issue was introduced into the Wisconsin legislature. In January, 1899, a resolution "relating to the health of old maids" was introduced by Assemblyman Henry L. Daggett, a farmer member from Bear Creek in Outagamie County. It was not printed in the *Journal*, but from newspaper accounts it would appear that it called for a joint committee to draft a bill prohibiting tight lacing. It was referred to by reporters as Daggett's "anti-lacing resolution."

Most of the newspapers quipped about the matter, treating it as one of those "diversions that serve to brighten the monotony of routine of charter-tinkering and Bear Creek bridging."

According to the Eau Claire *Daily Telegram,* "the resolution was introduced as a joke and the assemblymen are having all the fun out of it possible." That Daggett's fellow legislators did so regard it tends to be substantiated by the scanty record preserved in the *Assembly Journal.* There, in two brief entries, it is stated that Resolution 11A, "relating to the health of old maids," was referred successively to the Committee on Public Health and Sanitation, the Committee on Agriculture, and the Committee on Public Improvements! Of its final disposition no mention is made, nor is it included in the numerical list of resolutions appended to the published proceedings.

Yet I have been solemnly assured by several members of the 1899 legislature who are still living that the stout, chin-whiskered Daggett was entirely serious in his proposal, as were a considerable number of his colleagues. One may not assume, moreover, that he merely voiced the prejudices of his unsophisticated rural constituency. He was a man of some education and business experience. After acquiring a business college training, he had managed retail and wholesale stores for some years and had been the foreman of a freight depot at Fond du Lac before moving to Outagamie County in 1881 to start a dairy farm.

All the contemporary evidence suggests that Daggett was quite serious, and one suspects that he failed to appreciate the humor and jocularity his proposal evoked in the press. At a committee hearing where it was demonstrated that a woman could not speak above a whisper when encased in one of the corset contraptions of the day, Assemblyman Daggett shouted, "I don't wish to offend the ladies. But the evil is worse than the binding of the feet of Chinese women."

Throughout the session Daggett enjoyed the dubious prestige of widespread unpopularity and ridicule. A group of Watertown women presented him with a huge floral corset, tightly laced. The dance program for the legislative ball held on April 20, which was designed by Assemblyman Louie A. Lange, editor of the Fond du Lac *Daily Reporter*, showed Daggett as a knight with sword in hand about to launch an attack upon a monster corset, realistically drawn. At the bottom were two lines from Shakespeare (credited to Assemblyman Chris Sarau!): "Lay on, McDuff; and damned be him that first cries 'Hold, enough!'" Weeks before this, at the time of the legislative reception in late February, the press reported that Daggett's wife had become "so incensed at his notoriety that she refused to come to Madison to attend the reception."

At the close of the session the disillusioned Mr. Daggett returned to his home. But the lampooners were not yet done. On May 4 appeared the following item in the *New London Press*:

"This week Hon. Corset Daggett's plunder-box arrived at Bear Creek . . . a chest made in Madison for the legislators to store and carry home their stock of stationery, pencils, Blue books and other legislature papers. Daggett's was decorated upon the outside by pictures of handsome women in their nether garments, with waist enclosed in a certain brand of corsets. It attracted more attention at the Bear Creek station than a circus. There was a long string of people going to and from the depot to view the curiosity yesterday."

Serious-minded people used the episode as a point of departure for more sober reflections on the evil that Daggett sought to eradicate. One of them was the brilliant Amos P. Wilder, editor of the *Wisconsin State Journal*, whose son Thornton was later to achieve literary fame. While Daggett's resolution was still before the legislature Wilder wrote editorially that while the resolution itself was presumably not to be taken seriously, "it may not be amiss to say that the corset habit is on the decline. Especially in the cities where well-informed club and college-trained women to a great extent set the fashions, has the wasp-like waist gone glimmering among the things that were. In the rural districts misinformed young women still cramp and deform themselves into an abnormal, unhealthy and revolting parody on the beauty of the human form divine, unmindful of the official measurements of the faultless Venus de Milo (26 inches, if memory serves us right); and in the city, too, young women, especially of the sensational walks of life and those whose thought is too largely on appearances and not on the earnestness of an earthly mission, walk the streets with an attempt at neatness of form which misses the mark to all intelligent observers."

The medical profession, asserted Dr. Wilder, was united in its opposition to "the abhorrent practice." The "penalty paid in the experiences of motherhood is a terrific warning." Anyone who minimized that penalty had but to consult the books on the subject.

"But love of admiration," he conceded, "is the most powerful motive that controls the minds of a considerable portion of the weaker sex; and the most effective way of driving the corset into the limbo where the hoop-skirt and the slashed skirt continually do cry, is to convince women that there is nothing attractive or winning in any waist that is not anatomically correct.

"Mr. Daggett should beg leave to withdraw his bill, and substitute a resolution to the effect that no single man of the legislature is willing to entrust his hopes of connubial bliss to any home dominated by a woman who distorts her loveliness by artificial contrivances. As for the married men of the legislature, nothing they can say or do cuts any figure."

Mr. Daggett did not withdraw his resolution, but it was effectively smothered by the ridicule of colleagues and newsmen and the hostility of the women who resented being told by any man what they could or could not wear. Nor did he have another opportunity to carry on the crusade. Mr. Daggett was not among those present at the next session of the legislature.

Hot Stove Leagues: Brain
Trusters of Yesterday

AT HUSTISFORD, WHERE THE WATERS OF HORICON MARSH SPILL over the restraining dam to begin their course toward the valley of the Rock River, is an old-fashioned barbershop. For more than a half century townsmen and farmers round about have gathered within its walls in winter, and on benches outside in summer, to debate the affairs of state and nation and settle the problems of the moment. Like Banquo's ghost, these problems never down, but arise each day for fresh decisions.

Hustisford holds fast to the historic past. Its barbershop is one of the last of those places—which once included the country store and the livery stable—where for three score years after the Civil War men gathered, smoked, chewed, argued, and made decisions—complacent in the conviction that theirs was the true

51

vision of the nation's destiny. Presidents and governors might toss restlessly throughout the night seeking to resolve confusion into wise decisions. Not the Hot Stove Leaguers of Wisconsin. Nightly after their debates they returned home wondering why troubled executives failed to recognize the right path, which to them seemed as plainly marked as the shining planets overhead wheeling on their noiseless journey through the heavens.

Barbershop and country store have been modernized with the years. The old-time public forum has lost its appeal for younger generations, who seem less aware than did their forefathers of the issues influencing their lives. Only now and then does one find the ruins of a landmark: here a barbershop that still preserves the fancy shaving mugs of its customers, pigeonholed in a varnished case hanging on the wall; there a country store which still sells tea in bulk, gauges vinegar from the barrel, and measures ribbon and cloth from a yardage scale affixed to the counter.

Such a quaint shop is Paul Dornfeld's barbershop in Hustisford. Stories about it had been in the papers for years, and out of curiosity I visited it one day. The pastoral village lay snug and friendly, sunning itself after a long winter. As I opened the shop door I saw before me a cabinet of ornamental shaving mugs, and the gray-haired barber waiting at his chair. "They tell of the history of Hustisford," he began after learning of my interest in them. "I started this collection among my customers in 1895. Those were still the stagecoach days, and on these mugs are pictures of stage drivers, the first automobile owners, and men who worked at the trades around town or farmed in the country. Once I had as many as sixty mugs. Now the collection in use has dwindled to a third that number."

Mr. Dornfeld paused a moment to take down a mug. "This,"

he said, "is the mug that was owned by William Becker, who drove the stage to Woodland, six miles east, before automobiles were common." Suddenly his voice mellowed and his eyes assumed a faraway expression. "People had to be taken to Woodland to catch the train," he reminisced. "He used to make that trip twice a day. The picture on this mug shows him as a stage driver."

He handed me the mug to examine. Sure enough, it had on it a picture, painted in several colors, of a driver whipping up his horses as if to make up for lost time. "That figure in the driver's seat is William Becker, sure as life!" exclaimed the barber. "Afterward Becker bought one of the first automobiles to make these trips."

The trades, farming, and the fraternal lodges are represented in the pictures that adorn the shaving mugs in the Dornfeld collection. A. R. Grimm, who operated the first garage in the community, is shown standing beside his car; Ernest Zilisch, the tinsmith, as laboring with a repair job; and Paul Jeche with a threshing machine. Fred Lichtenberg, the cobbler, has a boot on his mug as a symbol of his craft. Most of the farmers' mugs depicted the heads of their favorite horses.

"The cups are going out of use," commented Barber Dornfeld as he put the last one back in its pigeonhole and turned to show me a heavy Wade and Butcher razor of early design. A razor is a beautiful thing in the hands of an old barber. Mr. Dornfeld showed me several which he kept in velvet cases in recognition of the good service they had given him. He went on to remark that barbers had been worried when the safety razor was introduced, but that their worry had proved to be needless. Many customers who had come to the shop only once or twice during the winter for a haircut and shave—total, thirty-five cents—now began coming in every two or three weeks for a haircut alone, for which they paid sixty-five cents.

Mr. Dornfeld chuckled over some early barbering methods. "Connected with the early-day barbershops was a bathroom. Ours is still in use. If it hadn't been for shops like mine, many people wouldn't have been able to take a bath after the river was frozen over, for it wasn't so long ago that the private home with a bath was a novelty. For the price of twenty-five cents in the early years, now thirty-five cents on weekdays, bathing privileges are afforded: a bath towel and a bar of soap, and take your turn. At one time many of the business people took a bath while waiting for a haircut, but the bathing end of the barbering business has declined."

So, too, has the interest in barbershop gatherings. This is attributable to the automobile and the radio, argues Mr. Dornfeld. Before their introduction the barbershop was a news center. There men gathered early in the day to learn what had happened during the past day or two. With the coming of fall the interest in politics was quickened, and debates increased in number and intensity. But it was chiefly to hear the news that most visitors dropped into the barbershop. Mr. Dornfeld had one of the first telephones, and many a man, he said, dropped in on the pretext of making a call when actually he wanted to listen in on the conversation of others. "I thought when the telephone came that a fellow in business could just sit down and watch the world go by. But if the next hundred years bring as many changes as the past I wonder what will happen to the business of barbering."

It was still early in the day when I concluded my interview with Mr. Dornfeld. My imagination fired with pictures of scenes past and gone, I decided to investigate the haunts of the Eel Pot Club barbershop and Prien's store at Columbus. These too had been notable gathering places for men who regarded argument and settlement of national affairs as part of their civic duty.

The Eel Pot, rendezvous of the professional and better-educated men of the community, might almost be said to have had a national membership. By 1885 its reputation was no longer merely local. Visitors from other states came in to listen to the disputations. It so chanced that many of its members had been born in New England and New York in the year 1819, the birth year of Queen Victoria—a coincidence in which they took great pride and which won them the nickname "the boys of nineteen."

One of the Eel Pot's daily visitors was a well-educated blind man, to whom the barber would read the newspaper when he was not busy at the chair. Soon this practice attracted others. When the train arrived and the daily paper was received, it was really read—not the headlines merely but down one column and then the next. No item was inconsequential enough to be skipped. With the reading of the last article the discussion began, Republicans and Democrats pitted against one another on the subject of political reform, the sinuosities of railroad-lumberman control of government, and other topics of the day. A frequent participant was former Governor James T. Lewis, a local resident, who was usually present whenever he was in town. Heated words were sometimes spoken in the course of the argument, but rarely did they affect the friendships of the group.

For those who spoke German the nearby Prien and Mirow store was another popular gathering place. Here the discussions were likely to be about national aspects of Old World history in their relation to American politics. Many of those who came here were former officers and soldiers of the Franco-Prussian

War, and they were occasionally referred to derisively as "John Prien's Standing Army." The disputations led by this and other foreign groups, however, had a far-reaching effect. Those who participated came to have a better understanding of the American way of life, which they imparted to their children. Many of their sons and daughters have since become leaders in their communities and in the state.

A retired salesman, Leo A. Kleiner of Madison, volunteered to take me over the route he had traveled years before in visiting his customers, that I might acquaint myself with the role which the country store had played in the hegemony of Wisconsin. The store of early days was more than a market and a salesroom; it was a social institution. Like the barbershop, it was the scene of a debating forum. The men who sat around the pot-bellied stoves, enveloped by clouds of smoke, acquired a knowledge and understanding of political life that helped to give the state of Wisconsin a genuinely democratic popular government.

Typical of these stores was the shop of the Howe Brothers in the Norwegian community of Stoughton. Saturday was the busiest day of the week. In the afternoon customers brought in baskets of eggs, all sizes, and crocks and jars of homemade butter, the color of which ranged from white to golden yellow. Scarcely noticing the group already gathered around the stove, a Norwegian farmer would enter, deposit his crates on the counter, and begin to fumble in his pockets.

"By golly!" he would exclaim. "The wife gave me a slip." And apologetically he would go through his clothes again while the busy clerk waited patiently. "Oh, here it is. Put these things up and give me a due bill for the balance." No prices were asked.

Then, noticing old friends from Telemarken and Goss in Old Norway seated about the stove, he would find a keg for himself and prepare to join in the argument. But not before he had taken out his pipe, glanced about, and asked, "Where is the poor box?" The man who held the floor simply pointed to the place where the storekeeper had deposited a well-filled container of Standard smoking tobacco, to which all present might help themselves. The clerks meantime hustled and bustled about filling orders.

Merchandise was quite differently arranged than it is in the modern store. Back of the counter were large barrels of sugar and crackers and boxes of prunes, dried peaches, apricots, and apples. Toward the rear was a hogshead of molasses or sorghum; so many turns of a crank measured out a gallon. Nearby were several open boxes containing different brands of plug tobacco with a device for cutting off the desired length. The shelves were filled with orange-colored packages of smoking tobacco; tinfoil-wrapped packages of Plowboy smoking tobacco lay next to boxes of saleratus (baking soda), cans of salmon, and bottles of vanilla extract. From the ceiling hung milk pails, lanterns, and manure forks. In the corner stood axes and ax-handles, shovels and spades. Eggs in baskets cluttered the floor. Toward the front were shelved packages of Arbuckle and McLaughlin (XXXX) coffee. In a showcase were stick licorice, horehound candy, peppermint discs, cone-shaped chocolate drops, rock candy, and spruce and blackjack gum. In the basement, in mingled disorder, were barrels of salt pork, dill pickles, vinegar and kerosene, a stack of lutefisk piled like cordwood, and a storeroom of supplies.

Many traveling salesmen planned their itinerary so that they might spend the night at the Hutson House in Stoughton. The proprietor, William S. Wood, was a genial host. Not only did he set a good table but he kept on hand a supply of fur coats, which he lent to salesmen who had to make trips by sleigh to the inland communities. Later other hotels and even livery stables offered this fur-coat service.

Stoughton was one of the communities where in the late nineties traveling men would be sure to find the Hot Stove League in session at the country store. Once their orders were listed, they hastened over to listen, either at the Howe Brothers or, if the debates there were not lively enough, at the J. B. Haven Store. It was an era of crusades of one sort and another and of widespread muckraking. The senior Robert M. La Follette was making his fight for the governorship, and "La Folletteism" was in the air. More than any other political figure in the state La Follette became the topic of country-store debates. The Norwegian element, which predominated in Dane County, embraced his ideas enthusiastically and became the backbone of his political progress. He became their idol, and it was their vote more than that of any other group which put him in office and supported his economic program.

As Mr. Kleiner and I traveled the route where nearly fifty years before he had taken orders in the daytime and listened in on discussions and arguments at night, he recounted many interesting bits of forgotten history.

"Every six weeks," he began, "I left Madison on Monday and went to Lancaster. On Monday afternoons I took orders at Lancaster and made arrangements at the livery stable to be driven in different directions so that I might canvass all the inland stores. It cost four dollars a day for a livery and driver.

"At night we sometimes stayed at hotels in off-the-railroad towns. The price of supper, bed, and breakfast was a dollar and a half. I was awakened early in the morning by the night clerk pounding on the door and calling to me that he was putting a pitcher of hot water just outside the door. I dressed and went downstairs.

"I can still smell those big breakfasts. The hotels of that day were operated on the American plan and you got all you could eat, and more. There was a bowl of oatmeal and cream. The oatmeal had been cooking for several hours and had a flavor never equaled by these three-minute preparations of today. Then came bacon and eggs, stacks of toast, cakes made the old-fashioned way, a dish of prunes, and coffee. There was a special table for travelers in these country hotels, which was called the transient table. At each end of it stood a bowl of fruit, mostly oranges. Farmers and workmen ate at other tables. Salesmen paid fifty cents for their meal; others, thirty-five cents. The traveling man's breakfast was one that was sure to bring him back on every visit."

Mr. Kleiner reminded me that the sale of cigarettes was at that time illegal. Most salesmen bootlegged on the side, at five cents a package, a brand known as Sweet Caporals. Inside each package was a picture of an opera star dressed in tights. Lillian Russell was the favorite, to be carried clandestinely by youthful smokers in the inside coat pocket. Cigarette smokers who preferred the Sweet Caporal brand sought to assemble the whole collection of twenty-four near-to-nude beauties.

"In those days," observed Mr. Kleiner, "cigarette-smoking was indulged in only by the few. But most of the men who gathered nightly at the country store chewed tobacco. For their convenience four or five low boxes filled with ashes were kept within the stove circle. In my five-day sales trips out of Lancaster I never sold less than six thousand pounds of smoking tobacco, and I sometimes sold as much as fourteen thousand pounds of plug tobacco. And there were other salesmen working this territory at the same time."

Dusk was spreading its mantle over the landscape when we reached Belleville. We had one stop more to make: at the former Denton J. Smith store a few miles out, on the road to Mount Vernon. As we approached the place, it suggested to me the pictures I had seen of country grocery stores before the Civil War. Lonely it stood by the roadside, its only companion an old oak tree. No great flight of the imagination was required to put one on the lookout for a recklessly driven stagecoach.

The kerosene lamps, which were already lighted, cast long shadows upon the road. The door opened with the stiffness of decrepitude, as if it were weary after almost a century's service. One quick glance about and I knew that my quest for the most old-fashioned country store in Wisconsin was ended. The clerk, dressed as an ordinary laborer, seèmed amused when I told him I had come in only to take a look. His amusement changed to pleasure as my eager eyes drifted from ceiling to shelves.

He gave me permission to step behind the counter and examine the faded boxes of patent medicines stowed there. Much of the printing on the wrappers had grown dim with age, but I could read the labels for Schiloh System Vitalizer, Dr. Shoop's Rheumatic Remedy, Pisol's for Coughs and Colds, Ramon's Pink Pills, Triner's Cough Sedative, Chamberlain's Balm-A Liniment, Parker's Hair Balsam, Allen's Foot-Ease.

"You must see our ladies' shoes," the beguiling clerk interrupted, leading me farther behind the counter. "Here is a fine pair of high-topped ladies' lace shoes that sells for seven dollars and a half." I held the article musingly, wondering whether the clerk might not offer to reduce the price. "It is a Selz brand," he volunteered, "well made."

Taking the shoe from me, he next showed me some button shoes and patent-leather shoes with cloth tops. He soon saw, however, that I was not a prospective purchaser. He closed the boxes and put them back on the shelves. "They still sell occasionally," he murmured.

"How long has this store been in operation?" I inquired.

"My father purchased it forty-eight years ago," he replied, "and it had been running for a long time before that."

"Do you have any opportunities to sell out?" I pressed.

"Several have wanted to buy it to start a tavern. But I don't like taverns. There are too many of them. The store is good enough for us. It has always been like this."

The conversation drifted to a discussion of hours of work. The clerk, Robert Smith, explained that it opened at half past seven in the morning to accommodate the truckers and remained open until half past eight or nine o'clock in the evening.

"Must you file an income-tax return for the store?" I ventured, hoping to learn more about the volume of trade.

"No," he responded, apparently amused. "Business is not as good as that."

Like a ghostly reminder of the evenings long ago when Denton J. Smith first operated the store and the farmers came in after the chores were done, the stools and chairs had been arranged in order around the stove, already red-hot from overheating. Bumps in the uneven floor were mute evidence of the thousands of feet that had walked across it.

"The chairs are waiting for the past to come back," I suggested as I rose to leave.

"The chairs are always vacant," said the clerk. His words went with me like an echo on the night's wind.

These stores are representative of all the country stores of the early days. To make them look impressive most of them were built with a square false front like the village stores of New England and New York in the mid-nineteenth century. As late as 1910 every old-fashioned country store was still a lively debating center. And it was to these very men who had argued and thought things out at country-store and barbershop gatherings that political power fell when the old system of caste and convention disintegrated in Wisconsin.

Their views were definitely tinged with idealism. It has been said, for instance, that all but a few of the men in the 1911 state legislature were of sufficiently high caliber to serve in the United States Senate. Its record would seem to support that assertion. No state, historians say, has contributed more ideas to good government and more patterns for national legislation than Wisconsin. The Hot Stove Leaguers were the rst brain trusters, albeit they little suspected how significant was their role.

There was a time in Wisconsin's history when men sought office for the honor inherent in it. They represented a grass-roots type of public official which is fast disappearing. Today the salary has become an important consideration for many. Few feel that they can accept a public position for the honorarium formerly paid. In the spring of 1946, for example, it was hard to find candidates for many minor positions in the towns and cities of the state because the salaries were too low to attract them.

The Wisconsin legislator now receives five times as much as he did in 1911. One result of this increase in the salaries of the chief elective officials of the state has been to attract more well-educated men. In 1945 two-thirds of the state's senators and half the assemblymen were men who had had some college training. Public administration has become a profession, to which, perhaps, less glamour attaches than in the olden days.

The Poor Man's Club: Free Lunches and Nickel Beers

THE OLD-TIME SALOON WAS THE POOR MAN'S CLUB. MEN GATHERED in the barbershop or sat around the country-store stove to discuss politics, but for good-fellowship, friendliness, and *Gemütlichkeit* they went to the saloon. To it came men from all walks of life. Within its portals a democratic spirit reigned, and all present became equals.

Standing at the bar with one foot on the rail or sitting around tables, little coteries talked companionably of their families and homes and of their work. They drank a little beer, ate of the free lunch, and then went home or back to their work. Social life today offers few meeting places like the old German saloon. Compared with it, the modern tavern is an arrogant pretender.

Beer had become a favorite American beverage before the

close of the Civil War. It had been introduced by the pioneers of German stock who could not accustom themselves to the hard liquors imbibed by some of the other races. With the increase of Teutonic immigration the drinking of beer became a social custom, the saloon a community center. Wherever a goodly number of Germans settled, there a brewery was likely to be established. The ease with which hops and barley could be raised on Wisconsin soil was an important factor in the growth of the industry.

Milwaukee became the chief center of manufacture. Even before lager beer began to be made there a brewery for the manufacture of ale had been established by a Welsh immigrant, Richard G. Owens. This was located at the foot of Huron Street (East Clybourn Street), where the waters of Lake Michigan washed up beside the basement walls. Its product was an ale of high alcoholic content that was popular with Welsh immigrants. The rapidly increasing German population, however, preferred lager beer with its lower alcoholic content, and eventually the market for ale virtually disappeared. The brewery established by Owens ceased to be a profitable enterprise and in 1880 went out of existence.

Before the Civil War the consumption of beer was confined largely to the Germans, whose national drink it had been in the Old World. Thereafter it became more popular among other nationalities, the wartime fraternization of soldiers having dispelled many of the prejudices against foreign customs. The low excise rates, as compared with the heavy taxation of ardent spirits in 1862, helped to promote the sale of beer.

The failure of the hop crop in New York in 1861 stimulated a ten-year craze of hop-growing in Sauk County, Wisconsin. For a time this county raised more than a fifth of all the hops grown in the country, a single year's profit being in excess of a million and a half dollars. Such an impetus did the manufacture of beer receive in Milwaukee that the names of some of its leading brewers continue to be recognized trademarks of our own generation: Captain Frederick Pabst, Joseph Schlitz, Valentin Blatz, and Adam Gettelman. Custom, fashion, and price combined to make it more respectable to drink beer than hard liquor. Not until the bootleg era of prohibition was the public taste for the lighter beverage to wane and the saloon to disappear, probably forever. Today's "tavern" bears so little resemblance to the saloon that it can scarcely be said to be a direct descendant.

The neighborly spirit of the Germans, who began to settle in Milwaukee in the 1830's and who came by the thousands after the Revolution of 1848, won for the city its reputation as the nation's *Hauptstadt* of *Gemütlichkeit* and worldwide acclaim as the Munich of America. As late as 1910 nearly seventy per cent of its population was of German birth or descent.

Gemütlichkeit was a characteristic of the saloon, especially the neighborhood saloon, in the horse-and-buggy days of the late nineteenth century. It served as a social center, and presently sociologists began to refer to it as the "poor man's club." The term is said to have been used early in the nineties by Professor Charles Zuebelin of Northwestern University. "The saloon is the poor man's club," he told a Milwaukee audience. "There is nothing wrong with the saloon except some of the uses that are made of it."

Even so, the term Poor Man's Club is something of a misnomer, for the saloon attracted not only the daily worker, but his employer and the business and professional men of the community, many of whom were men of wealth. What the term implied, of course, was that the saloon's clientele was not drawn from the highbrow or social-register classes. Nor was its locale confined to Milwaukee. Every city in the state from Superior to Kenosha, from Green Bay to La Crosse, had such gathering places. Neighborhood clubs also sprang up in cigar stores and other shops, but they thrived especially well in the saloon, where the beer and the free lunch fostered conviviality.

The Poor Man's Club was born of men's desire, conscious or unconscious, for friendly relations with their neighbors. It existed without formal organization, recorded membership, officers, or funds for planned activities. No class cleavages were recognized, characteristic as these were of German society. In general the German who could boast a "Von" prefix in his name was looked up to by those who could not; occasionally it was remarked of a woman who came into the old West Side Turner Hall for a Sunday concert or entered the old Deutsches Club that "she's a two-times 'Von.'" But in the popular gathering places—the Schlitz Palm Garden, Schlitz Park, the Milwaukee Garden, Heiser's—the measuring stick of wealth and family prestige was not applied. Rich and poor, artist and laborer, scholar and illiterate all mingled as a single family united by the bonds of homeland and community of tastes.

The saloon supplied the beer which mellowed the discussion of personal, family, state, and national problems. For the price of a nickel one could get a big glass of beer and a substantial lunch and stay as long as he liked. Neighborhood saloonkeepers were usually assisted by their wives and daughters, and before long the men began to be joined at their impromptu club by their wives and other feminine members of the family. When this became common a "Family Entrance" to the saloon was provided. This innovation greatly interested visitors from other cities and gave Milwaukee its reputation as the only American

city that welcomed housewives to its saloons. It was often re-marked that their presence had a salutary effect on the deport-ment of their menfolk.

The Poor Man's Club was necessarily an orderly affair, es-pecially after families were admitted. They gave the police little trouble until the sale of hard liquor began to increase and ob-jectionable features were introduced which eventually resulted in curfews, specified closing hours, and other restrictive legisla-tion.

Throughout the Gay Nineties beer was cheap, the tax on it being negligible. Indeed it was not until 1944 that the five-cent glass of beer became scarce in Milwaukee. During the late nine-ties there were four saloons on the southwest corner of State and Third streets which sold two beers for a nickel and provided an elaborate free lunch of roast beef, baked ham, sausage, baked beans, vegetables, salads, bread and butter, and other appetizing foods. Two men with but a nickel between them could each en-joy a substantial meal and a mammoth beer.

The early Poor Man's Club solved an important social-eco-nomic problem. In a time when capital was needed for the building of homes and the promotion of commercial and indus-trial activities it provided recreation and social intercourse for almost nothing. True, there were also the *Turnvereins,* devoted to the teaching of gymnastics and the cultivation of the mind. But not all residents of a neighborhood were turners. For those who were not, the saloons and beer gardens offered a wide range of entertainment.

Largest of the early beer gardens was the Milwaukee Garden, which occupied a three-acre tract on the outskirts of the city, now the block bounded by Highland Avenue and State, Four-teenth, and Fifteenth streets. This "beautiful and elegant sum-

mer garden," established during the 1850's, was a glorified Poor
Man's Club. It accommodated ten thousand patrons and made
a specialty of entertainment: concerts, plays, dancing, bowling,
and other sports. On the grounds, which were lighted by three
hundred gas lamps, was a menagerie, a large restaurant which
during the summer months served patrons out of doors, and a
midway with wheels of fortune, refreshment stands, and numerous stalls selling souvenirs of one sort and another.

Schlitz Park, originally known as Quentin's Park, was taken
over by the Schlitz Brewing Company in 1879. For a quarter
of a century thereafter it was Milwaukee's most popular beer
garden. On top of a hill in the center of the eight-acre tract at
North Eighth and Walnut streets stood a pagoda that overlooked
the entire city. Elsewhere on the grounds were a concert hall
having a capacity of five thousand, a large restaurant, winter
dance hall, menagerie, and bowling alleys. "It is the finest Summer Resort in the country," ran its advertisement in a Milwaukee guidebook of 1886. "View of the City from Lookout Hill
unrivalled. Best Restaurant in the City. Its beautiful shady walks
and flower-beds, its grotesque fountains unsurpassed. Grand
splendor at night when ablaze with its 32 electric lights, 500
colored gas globes, and thousands of gas flames. You can not
say you have seen Milwaukee if you have failed to pay homage
to Schlitz Park." Every year hundreds of thousands of men,
women, and children passed through its arched portal to the
innumerable attractions awaiting young and old.

In 1896 the most notable of the indoor "palm gardens" was
opened. This was the world-famous Schlitz Palm Garden next
to the Schlitz Hotel at Grand Avenue (West Wisconsin Avenue)
and North Third Street. Despite its impressive architecture and
the splendor of its appointments—vaulted ceiling, pipe organ,

stained-glass windows, potted palms, and rich oil paintings—
the Schlitz Palm Garden may also be called a Poor Man's Club.
For no class distinctions were recognized here. The lowly were
made to feel as welcome as the rich; no patron was given espe-
cial consideration simply because he spent liberally. As often as
not a poor man and his wife would be seated next to a table of
some of the city's "best people."

In the big barroom from thirty to fifty barrels of beer was dispensed daily, at five cents a glass, and free lunches were provided as in other saloons of the day. On Sunday afternoons
whole families came to listen to a concert given by the Garden's
own company of red-jacketed musicians, by the Milwaukee
Musical Society, or by some nationally known organization such
as Creatore's Band, Pryor's Band, or the orchestra conducted by
the renowned Christopher Bach. The acrobatic Italian maestro
Giuseppe Creatore, cavorting before his bandsmen and tossing
his heavy mane of hair, never failed to delight his audience.

The tavern at 503 North Plankinton Avenue has for more than
a half century been another Poor Man's Club, though it has also
been patronized by some well-known men, among them Governor George W. Peck, famous as the author of *Peck's Bad Boy*.
Today it is operated by Theodore A. Thomas, son of the man
who founded it in the eighties and who was a leading spirit
among gun-club enthusiasts until his death in 1920. This tavern,
probably the last of its kind in the state, typifies the Poor Man's
Club of former days. Its patrons are largely workers and small
employers. A huge stove in the center of the room still functions
as heating plant as it did sixty years ago.

The Wayside Inn at 1 Northwestern Lane, the alley between
East Wisconsin Avenue and East Michigan Street midway between North Water and Broadway, was another modest place

which for fifty years before its demolition in 1946 had been a favorite rendezvous of men from many fields of endeavor. It had been built in 1876 by one Colonel John Harper, who disappeared after its completion, inspiring countless suspicions and conjectures. His successor was John Gallagher, who would serve no patron more than two drinks, on the ground that if he wanted more than two he was not a gentleman and was therefore unwelcome at the Wayside. Apparently, however, his ostracism extended no further. During his proprietorship the place became the favorite haunt of Mayor David Rose and his political cohorts, many of whose deals with corporations are reputed to have originated in a rear booth of the saloon.

With prohibition and repeal came a series of proprietors, the last of whom was Robert "Barney" Fredericks, connoisseur of wines, collector of curios, and music-lover. The Wayside now became the rendezvous of a quite different coterie. Writers of mystery stories gathered here to hatch their plots for the pulp magazines; painters brought their subjects for a few drinks before making preliminary portrait sketches; and commercial artists and their co-workers met to talk over illustrations for advertising copy. On designated nights a small group of regular patrons gathered to listen to the collection of records that Barney had stowed under the bar: Bach, Brahms, Chopin, Strauss, and Tchaikovsky. They turned a cold shoulder on intruders who came merely out of curiosity and made a disturbance by talking and moving about. The story is told that on one evening when the place was jammed with such casual customers, nobody was served and the records remained in their cabinet all evening. By such tactics the habitués froze out unwelcome visitors and reestablished their exclusive "concert" nights.

Another establishment which limited the customer to two

drinks was Judge Sholes's white saloon on the north side of Michigan Street between Second and Third. Portly Judge Sholes —that was the only name he acknowledged—was a man of mystery. None knew where he had come from, and no relatives were to be found when he died. Lowly patrons received from him the same consideration he gave to more influential men. As a customer was leaving the bar Judge Sholes invariably invited him to "call again." His place was a comfortable one, especially cheerful during the winter months when a blazing fire was kept burning in the fireplace.

Perhaps the most popular of the downtown bars and restaurants, the most cosmopolitan of the clubs interested in social and political problems, was Weber and Stuber's just east of the river near Wisconsin Avenue. During the nineties and early years of the twentieth century it was a rendezvous for members of all political parties. If one wanted to learn what was going on in the world of politics, he went there to find out. Upon entering, and sometimes upon leaving, he received a hearty handshake from the late Henry Weber, who probably had shaken hands with more people than any other man in Milwaukee.

A score of other saloons and beer gardens were famous during the nineties and thereafter for their food and drink, entertainment, and social atmosphere. Among them were Pabst Park, formerly Schuetzen or Shooting Park, between North Third and Fifth streets south of Burleigh, whose attractions included a fifteen-thousand-foot roller coaster, a Katzenjammer Palace of fun and hilarity, Wild West shows, and daily summer concerts; Francis Lackner's Terrace Garden on Prairie Street (West Highland Avenue) at North Ninth Street, which later became the site of Trinity Lutheran Church; Mother Heiser's more modest but highly popular tavern at North Jackson Street and East

Ogden Avenue, where in summer food and drink were served outdoors and where a table was reserved inside for the group of German brewers, lithographers, and newspapermen whose earnest discussions gave the place its nickname "The Reichstag"; Busch's at the west end of the North Avenue bridge, accessible by steamboat and rowboat; other riverbank gardens, such as Pleasant Valley Park, opened in 1870, and Lueddemann's on the River, from the grounds of which customers could watch the river regattas; Lueddemann's on the Lake, later converted into the present Lake Park; the Pabst resort, originally Isenring's, at Whitefish Bay, which became nationally famous for its planked whitefish; the Kuenstlerheim ("Artists' Home") at West Water Street (North Plankinton Avenue) and West Wells Street, which was the haunt of painters, actors, and others of Bohemian temperament and tastes; and the bars of the leading hotels, such as the Republican, the Kirby, the Pfister, and the old Plankinton.

The free lunches of the old days included all manner of foods, variously prepared. At the bar of the Hotel Pfister champagne ham was offered with beer at exactly four o'clock every afternoon. At the Egg House at North Water and East Mason streets a raw or hard-cooked egg was served with every glass of beer, ten crates a day being required to meet the demand. The Oyster Bar on Wisconsin Avenue near North Second Street offered three oysters, fried or raw, with every drink. The Pancake, on North Plankinton Avenue, served two hot potato pancakes with each nickel glass of beer. For this purpose the proprietor's wife peeled two bushels of potatoes daily.

"Back in 1908," an old newspaperman has confided to me, "I was young and broke, but filled with the conviction that I was the smartest reporter in the state out of a job. For weeks I tramped in and out of city rooms hoping to get an assignment. Had it not been for the stacks of potato pancakes and other delicacies on the free-lunch counters of numerous saloons I would have been forced to creep home a disillusioned and very unhappy kid. As it was, I did little 'eating jobs' on the old *Free Press* and finally landed on the *Sentinel*."

One of the imposing spectacles of the saloon era in Milwaukee was the delivery of kegs and barrels of beer. These were hauled in sturdily built wagons drawn by thoroughbred draft horses, groomed to perfection and wearing a shining harness glistening with metal decorations. The whole Northwest must have been searched for horses so perfectly matched. The arrival of these teams at delivery points attracted many onlookers, especially wide-eyed, curious children of the neighborhood. Like the wooden Indians that once stood in front of every cigar store, these splendid horses have passed out of the daily life of Milwaukee.

With improvements in transportation after the turn of the century, social conditions in Milwaukee, as elsewhere throughout the country, were greatly changed, and the neighborhood saloon became less important as a social institution. Fast and comfortable street railways and an increasing number of motor vehicles have for five decades been bringing the outskirts into ever closer touch with the night life attractions of downtown Milwaukee, its glamorous bars, its theaters and movie houses, and the cafes where one may dance to the music of nationally advertised orchestras. Despite all these changes, however, the neighborhood tavern continues to serve the community as a social center.

In northern Wisconsin saloons were operated somewhat differently than elsewhere in the state. At Antigo, Merrill, Tomahawk, Rhinelander, Ashland, and other pinery towns, they clustered around the railway depot in order to catch the lumberjack as he came out of the woods in the spring. The saloonkeeper, having discounted the wage-credit slip of the lumber company ten per cent, which would not fall due until the logs reached the mills, would turn his saloon over to his customers. He made more money from the discounts than from the sale of liquor. Some of the lumberjacks charged that they had been robbed while they were intoxicated. However that may be, most of them were penniless within three weeks after their arrival in town.

Famous among the old-time free-lunch establishments were those that were operated at Madison for students, state employees, and legislators. Hausmann's and John Hamacher's in the Latin section were gathering places for many of the University boys; Joseph Wirka's and Fritz Genske's, on opposite sides of Capitol Square, for the politicians. In all of them the atmosphere was unmistakably German.

Especially popular with the students was Hamacher's, just west of the Capitol. Here a deep-brown bock beer was served in half-gallon, two-handled mugs. Hugging the tables in low grandfather chairs, the argumentative young collegians—some wearing their hair long for better protection on the football field—spent many a leisure hour in discussion. There was little talk about girls. During the fall the favorite topic was football and the pigskin heroes of the hour: Pat O'Dea, the Cochems brothers, Ikey Karel, Ed Vanderboom, Slam Anderson, Fred Kull, John Richards, and others. During the winter months it was the debating teams and their stars: William Kies, Albert Schmidt, Henry Lockney, Algie Simons, E. Ray Stevens, and George I. Haight. As the boys became convivial they started singing German songs: *O Tannenbaum, Auf Wiedersehen,* and many others. Many a poor boy would have had a hard time getting along on his meager allowance from home had it not been for Hamacher's and Hausmann's free lunches of calf liver and onions, beef and hot potatoes, bologna and pickles, sardines and coleslaw.

Many of the legislators, whose biennial salary was five hundred dollars in those days, also availed themselves of the saloons' free lunches. At mealtime they hurried over to Wirka's or Genske's, where a free lunch of cold meats, fish, cheese, and relishes awaited them, all to be had with a nickel glass of beer. No lobbyists hung about the Capitol corridors in those days awaiting the opportunity to invite the unsuspecting legislator to a pancake breakfast or a steak dinner. The German custom of the "Dutch treat"—each patron ordering and paying for himself—was usually followed. No restrictions were placed on the feasting, but both Wirka's and Genske's limited the serving of beer. When "unser Fritz," as Genske was popularly called, served a man his second glass, he wiped the bar before him and smilingly remarked "See you tomorrow!"

Among the more pretentious saloons that had a free-lunch counter was the Deutsches Dorf at Watertown, which came to enjoy a statewide reputation. Architecturally it was modeled upon the most famous German drinking place at the World's Fair held in St. Louis in 1904. With its carved woodwork it looked more like a music hall than a saloon, and it often served this purpose. Groups of patrons would join their voices in old German songs and ballads, and on special occasions the proprietor, Garret M. Gahlman, would bring a German orchestra from Milwaukee to entertain his customers. During the preprohibition era its massive oak bar, laden with a variety of good food, required the services of four attendants.

Good company, good discourse, and good music, these summon the best there is in man. All three were available at the old Poor Man's Club until excessive competition and the disregard of old ideals and amenities brought the institution into disrepute. And now it is gone forever.

A New Confection: Birth of the
Ice Cream Sundae

THE ICE CREAM SUNDAE WAS BORN OF HUMAN CURIOSITY. AMONG
the participants in the strange drama that gave America one of
its most popular confections were a cautious "soda parlor" proprietor, a hungry youth who liked ice cream, and a ten-year-
old girl who insisted that any day could be called Sunday.

It began back in 1881 in Two Rivers, Wisconsin, according
to local legend. There a modest ice cream store was operated
by Edward C. Berners, which had become a rendezvous for the
younger set in town. A dish of plain ice cream sold for five cents.
One night a customer, George Hallauer, ordered a dish and
while waiting for it asked the proprietor to "put some of that
chocolate syrup on it," pointing to a bottle of the sauce that was
used in the making of sodas.

"You don't want to ruin your dish of ice cream," admonished Mr. Berners; "I use that sauce only for sodas." Nevertheless he yielded and poured the rich thick syrup over the ice cream, meantime betraying on his countenance his sense of guilt and discomfiture. But George liked the new concoction and ordered a second dish. Others who stood about also tried it, and they too relished it. The next day was a busy one in the Berners soda parlor.

Presently confectioners in Manitowoc, six miles away, heard of the discovery. One of them, Charles W. Giffey, came over to Two Rivers to investigate. "What do you mean," he demanded of Mr. Berners, "by putting soda sauce on ice cream? The practice will ruin our business. It's giving too much for a nickel."

Giffey sat down at a table and Berners served him. Long before he had finished the dish Mr. Giffey's displeasure had vanished. Then the two of them sat down together and talked over the problem of cost. To one of them came a brilliant idea. They would make the new delicacy a sales leader. Only on Sunday would they serve the combination for a nickel.

Some days later a little girl came into the Giffey shop. She wanted some ice cream "with stuff on it."

"But we serve that only on Sunday," explained the proprietor.

"Then it must be Sunday," the child insisted, "because I want that kind." And she waited to be served.

The story soon went the rounds and presently everybody was calling the new goody a "Sunday." How or why the spelling was changed to "sundae" none of the principals seem to remember. Soon the glass manufacturers became interested and designed a special dish for it.

All sorts of combinations were tried. Customers demanded marshmallows, nuts, whipped cream, even a whole banana. Each

new mixture became a new sundae: the Jennie Flip, the Two Rivers, the Goldfish, the Sunshine. Every drugstore and confectionery shop named its own.

The first soda fountain in Wisconsin was probably that which Dr. Edward Johnson had installed in his drugstore in Watertown nearly forty years earlier. He had seen one in operation in the East, but had been without sufficient funds to purchase the device. Finally he manufactured one of his own design. According to his diary, which lay unread after his death until 1937, it was fashioned of tin, and pressure was obtained by means of a set of connections to the second floor of the store. At first the local trade did not like the tartaric drink, but gradually it caught on and became popular, though it was some time before the modern soda fountain was installed in drugstores generally.

Plain undecorated ice cream was of course "old stuff." It had been served in the courts of Europe since the late eighteenth century and had been introduced in the White House by Dolly Madison. As early as 1851 an American dairyman, Jacob Fussell, established an ice cream plant in the national capital and began to turn his excess milk into ice cream for delivery to his customers; a decade or so later he had opened ice cream plants in Baltimore, Boston, and New York. With the invention of the wooden "dasher" freezer the making of ice cream was brought into home kitchens and small confectionery shops throughout  America. By 1876, the year of the Centennial Exposition at Philadelphia, ice cream and ice cream sodas had become popular with many who visited the exposition. Before the close of the century ice cream was being widely manufactured in commercial plants, though still with hand-operated equipment.

The first malted milk ever drunk was made in Racine in 1883 by the late William Horlick. It soon became a commercial formula which years of advertising have made one of the most popular offerings of the soda fountain, though it has never displaced the ice cream soda. The soda, invented many years before the sundae, has remained a favorite, especially in college towns, where so many of the soft drinks have originated and been popularized. The milk shake, for example—a combination of milk, cracked ice, and sweetened flavoring—was for a decade before the Gay Nineties a favorite drink of students at the University of Wisconsin.

Lucien M. Hanks, Madison financier, relates how when a student he once took part in a milk-shake drinking contest at the old Lewis drugstore in Madison. "Milk shake was the popular student drink of those days," he said. "Perhaps as many as a dozen students participated in the contest. One, a little taller than I, won with the thirteenth glassful."

An Outmoded Industry: A Half Century of Ice Harvesting

THE SODA-FOUNTAIN BUSINESS COULD NOT HAVE DEVELOPED TO the proportions it did had it not been for another industry of the same day: the storage and sale of ice cut in winter. This made possible the manufacture of ice cream during the hot summer months, as well as the longer preservation of perishable foods, the cooling of beer and other drinks, the reduction of the temperature in mortuary parlors, and more comfortable railway travel. By 1869 the harvesting of ice from lakes, ponds, and streams of Wisconsin had become of sufficient importance to warrant the attention of the legislators. In that year a law was passed requiring all persons engaged in the removal of ice from surface water to enclose the opening with a fence "of brush or boards or other material."

Ten years later ice harvesters were enjoying a boom that was to continue for forty years, until the introduction of modern refrigeration. On all the principal lakes of the state large structures were erected in which vast quantities of ice were stored during the coldest winter months. After Christmas each year, when the thermometer usually dipped below zero, workmen gathered at the empty storage houses in search of a job at ice cutting; thousands of men were transported to northern Wisconsin from the larger cities. Like lumbering, it was a seasonal occupation requiring large crews for brief periods of four to six weeks. One Milwaukee ice company, for example, employed a thousand hands in winter, but only one hundred in summer. Unlike the present-day laborer who worries if he does not have steady employment, these workmen of fifty years ago seemed eager to take these short-term jobs and then move on to others elsewhere.

As soon as the ice was at least twenty-four inches thick a large square field was marked off into cakes two by four feet. An opening was made in the ice, and horse-drawn plows began cutting, first along the straight lines in one direction and then along the crossing lines. The blocks of ice were broken off with saws and picks and floated to the warehouse for storage or to freight cars for shipment. In the warehouses sawdust was packed between the cakes, and when the storage space was fully occupied the entire ice pack was covered with a coarse hay cut for the purpose. Much of this hay came from the marshes around Monches, Horicon, Waukau, and Green Bay.

Ice harvesting was a colorful and exciting enterprise. The workers dressed heavily and wore Scotch caps to protect their ears from the wintry blasts. They spoke a now-forgotten language as they called directions to their fellow workers. Occasionally a man would slip and fall into the water, and would have to be fished out and dried beside the fire which the workers kept burning as a refuge of warmth. Sometimes a team would break away, smash the fence enclosing the open waters, and drown in the deeps. Again one of the hoisting cables that elevated the cakes would snap, precipitating a long ribbon of ice back into the water and frightening out of their wits the men who with long poles were guiding the cakes to the hoist. At one of these spots life was exciting and swift in tempo. There were always more watchers than workmen.

Ice was harvested both for local consumption and for use in the larger cities of Wisconsin and other states. When the local storage houses were full, trainloads of ice were shipped to Chicago and neighboring cities from Lake Geneva, North Lake, Pewaukee Lake, the Madison lakes, Sturgeon Bay, Lake Winnebago, Random Lake, Lake Katherine, Rock Lake, and scores of others. Trainloads left Madison, often daily, for shipment via the Illinois Central to warehouses as far south as New Orleans and McComb, Mississippi. Trainload shipments were delivered to the packing houses and breweries of Milwaukee and Sheboygan from points as far north as Ashland. The Knickerbocker Ice Company of Chicago maintained at Madison, Sturgeon Bay, Lake Mills, and Lake Geneva tremendous storage houses from which they could make shipments in summer. The Pullman Car Company obtained from Wisconsin lakes most of the supply it used for icing cars. The Chicago and North Western published rates for shipments of ice from twenty-three points on its lines in Wisconsin lake regions, and the Chicago, Milwaukee, and St. Paul had an even longer list of tariffs. At Lake Geneva the wealthy Chicagoans who gathered there in summer exhausted every legal resource in an attempt to check the spoliation of the lake's beautiful shoreline. But the icehouses, unsightly as they were, meant too much to business to be summarily dispensed with.

The ice industry also created problems of public health. Laws were enacted prohibiting the removal of ice from specified areas of the Milwaukee River and Sturgeon Bay. Vendors distributing ice for household uses or impure ice for cooling purposes were required to post conspicuously on their wagons the name of the lake or stream from which their product had been cut. Local sanitation authorities in the larger cities like Milwaukee stressed the importance of purity and cleanliness, as did the leading distributors themselves. The Wisconsin Lakes Ice Company of Milwaukee, for example, boasted that all its ice was cut from "clear spring water lakes having no swamps or morasses and whose water contains the proper ingredients for the conservation of the health of the people."

The industry interested the legislators for other reasons also. They saw the possibility of deriving from it greatly increased revenues for the common schools. Arguing that title to the beds of the navigable lakes of Wisconsin was vested in the state, they maintained that the state might properly require licenses for the cutting of ice and thus establish a source of considerable revenue. A law to this end was enacted, only to be declared unconstitutional in 1902 by the state supreme court. Title to the beds of navigable waters, ruled the court, "is vested in the state in trust to preserve the same for the enjoyment of the people. The state has no proprietary right in such beds or in the water above the same, nor in the fish that inhabit such water or the fowls that resort thereto, or the ice that forms thereon, which it can deal in by sale or otherwise. When the term 'people of the state' is used to designate the beneficiaries of the trust in navigable waters, all the people who may choose to enjoy the same within the state are referred to, whether citizens of the state or persons who come within its territory for the purpose of enjoying such public rights." That decision marked a milestone. It has become the foundation of legislation that now vests in the public alone all the rights connected with Wisconsin's navigable lakes and streams.

For the ultimate collapse of the industry the businessmen of the state were unprepared, despite the progress that was being made in the field of mechanical refrigeration. As late as 1916 editors of agricultural journals were urging farmers to build icehouses to replace the outmoded pail-in-the-well method of cooling food and drink. For less than a dollar a ton, it was urged, twelve tons of ice could be harvested, enough to meet the needs of the average farm household for an entire summer. It looked as if the harvesting of ice offered real promise for the improvement of farm life.

Then came the crash. By 1920 carload shipments of ice to the South had been discontinued by the Illinois Central, and many of the huge icehouses on Wisconsin lakes were no longer needed. At Madison, one of the last communities to surrender, the industry struggled on until 1937. In a few isolated settlements and tourist camps winter storage of ice continues, but as a lucrative industry ice harvesting is dead. Dilapidated icehouse runways and mounds of rotting sawdust are all that remain to remind us of those roistering winter days of an enterprise that added its own bit of color and romance to the era, served its purpose, and then vanished forever.

They Knew "Old Abe": Wisconsin's Civil War Eagle

IF NOT THE MOST FAMOUS BIRD IN HISTORY, "OLD ABE," THE eagle that served as mascot for the Eighth Wisconsin Infantry in the Civil War, is unquestionably the best-known bird of modern times. In his many military engagements he was an unfailing fount of inspiration to the men with whom he shared war's rigors, and was twice wounded himself. When peace came he was by common consent accorded the distinction of having "never lost a battle."

Thereafter Old Abe became an emblem of Americanism. He was taken to reunions and community gatherings everywhere to inspire people to contribute to the care of disabled soldiers. At the sanitation fair held in Chicago in 1864 he was the attraction that raised sixteen thousand dollars for the cause corresponding to today's Red Cross. At the Republican convention which first nominated Ulysses S. Grant for the presidency he stood on his shield screaming for victory; at the Centennial Exposition at Philadelphia in 1876 more people came to see this bald eagle perched on his standard than to the demonstration of the telephone, which was just being introduced to the world.

When I came to Madison in 1902 as a university student and part-time newspaper reporter, there were still many Grand Army men working in the Capitol who had known Old Abe intimately, though the famous eagle had been dead for more than twenty years. I was fascinated by the stories of his feats of bravery that were related by Captain Hosea W. Rood, William J. McKay, Captain M. J. Rawson, and others who were to write many articles on this veteran bird's activities. Since then I have garnered every scrap of information available about this famous mascot of Union troops in the war between the states. When later I stood on the shores of Island Lake near Weyerhaeuser, Wisconsin, I envisioned the majesty of the emerald pine atop Flambeau Hill where the fledgling was taken from its nest in the spring of 1861.

Old Abe was captured by Chief Sky, an Indian of the Lac du Flambeau band of Chippewa. A few days later, at the pioneer home of Daniel McCann ten miles up the Chippewa River from Chippewa Falls, Mrs. McCann bartered the bird, then no larger than a crow, for a bag of corn. But she soon regretted the deal. Her husband, annoyed because of the care the bird required, took him to Eau Claire and sold him for two dollars and a half to a group of soldiers who were about to leave for Camp Randall at Madison.

From that day forward the bird had a role in American history. The soldiers christened him "Old Abe" and changed the name of their company to "The Eagles." Before long the regiment to which the company belonged was to become famous as the Wisconsin Eagles.

A perch in the form of a shield was fashioned for Old Abe, on which were painted the stars and stripes and the inscription "8th Reg. W. V." The perch was mounted on a five-foot pole. The bearer, by setting the staff in a belt-socket, held up the bird at a station assigned to him at the very center of the line of march, beside the flag.

Everywhere the fame of Old Abe preceded the regiment. He was formally sworn into the United States service and bedecked in red, white, and blue ribbons. Madison women presented the regiment with a metal perch for the bird. A businessman of St. Louis offered to buy him for five hundred dollars. But the bird was not for sale.

Abe soon received his baptism of fire and thereafter participated in many engagements, including the tough battle fought at Farmington, Mississippi, in May, 1862. After he had overcome his initial surprise the bird seemed to catch the spirit of battle and screamed fiercely, especially when the company advanced. Thereafter he always showed great interest when the company made preparations to move. When an engagement opened he would jabber raucously and occasionally soar around as if scouting, then return to his perch and call noisily as if urging the men to action. So stimulating an effect did the bird have on the morale of the Union soldiers that they came to believe that his very presence was an omen of victory. One Confederate general is said to have remarked that he would rather capture the "sky buzzard" than a whole brigade of soldiers.

Hundreds of volunteers of the Eagle regiment were killed in battle or died of wounds or disease, but Old Abe returned from the war hale and hearty, despite several years of hardships and two battle wounds, inflicted at Corinth and Vicksburg. On September 22, 1864, the soldiers marched through the streets of Madison carrying Old Abe bobbing on his perch. He received a greater ovation than the men themselves and seemed to enjoy every voice of welcome. Occasionally he would flap his wings as a special token of recognition.

After the homecoming celebrations were over Old Abe was presented to the state of Wisconsin. Now he was honored in quieter fashion. He was given a room in the basement of the Capitol, and a soldier comrade became his private caretaker. He continued to be a great attraction. Everyone wanted to see the famous war eagle that had gone through so many battles, spurred so many soldiers on to victory. His moulted feathers sold for five dollars apiece. When the supply was exhausted, so the story goes, matching chicken feathers were substituted.

Old Abe became an active member of the Grand Army of the Republic and attended army reunions, patriotic celebrations, dedicatory exercises, and political rallies and conventions. He was taken to New York, Boston, Philadelphia, Detroit, Chicago, and other cities. The sale of his picture brought in thousands of dollars for the relief of disabled soldiers. P. T. Barnum was ready to spend twenty thousand dollars to obtain him as a circus attraction, but neither his nor any other offer was ever seriously entertained. In 1876, by a special act of the legislature and with the approval of the governor, Old Abe was exhibited at the Centennial Exposition at Philadelphia. On most of these tours Abe's chaperone was Johnny Hill, who before the Civil War had lived within sight of the eagle's treetop birthplace and who had enlisted with him at Eau Claire in 1861.

Stories that now seem almost legendary are told of the thousands of people who with their children made special trips to Madison to visit Old Abe. A touching description of one child's visit has been left us by Jane Addams of Hull House fame, whose early home was at Cedarville, Illinois, north of Freeport.

"My childish admiration for Lincoln," wrote Miss Addams in later years, "is closely associated with a visit made to the war eagle, Old Abe, who, as we children well knew, lived in the state capitol of Wisconsin, only sixty-five miles north of our house, really no farther than an eagle could easily fly! He had been carried by the Eighth Wisconsin Regiment through the entire war, and now dwelt an honored pensioner in the state building itself.

"Many times, standing in the north end of our orchard, which was only twelve miles from that mysterious line which divided Illinois from Wisconsin, we anxiously scanned the deep sky, hoping to see Old Abe fly southward right over our apple trees, for it was clearly possible that he might at any moment escape from his keeper, who, although he had been a soldier and a sentinel, would have to sleep sometimes. We gazed with thrilled interest at one speck after another in the flawless sky, but although Old Abe never came to see us, a much more incredible thing happened, for we were at last taken to see him.

"But although Old Abe, sitting sedately upon his high perch, was sufficiently like an uplifted ensign to remind us of a Roman eagle, and although his veteran keeper, clad in an old army coat, was ready to answer all our questions and to tell us of the thirty-six battles and skirmishes through which Old Abe had passed unscathed, the crowning moment of the impressive journey came to me later, illustrating once more that children are as quick to catch the meaning of a symbol as they are unaccountably slow to understand the real world about them.

"The entire journey to the veteran war eagle had itself symbolized that search for the heroic and perfect which so persistently haunts the young; and as I stood under the great white dome of Old Abe's stately home, for one brief moment the search was rewarded. I dimly caught a hint of what men have tried to say in their world-old effort to imprison a space in so divine a line that it shall hold only yearning devotion and high-hearted hopes. Certainly the utmost rim of my first dome was filled with the tumultuous impression of soldiers marching to death for freedom's sake, of pioneers streaming westward to establish self-government in yet another sovereign state. Only the great dome of St. Peter's itself has ever clutched my heart as did that modest curve which had sequestered from infinitude in a place small enough for my child's mind, the courage and endurance which I could not comprehend so long as it was lost in 'the void of unresponsive space' under the vaulting sky itself. But through all my vivid sensations there persisted the image of the eagle in the corridor below and Lincoln himself as an epitome of all that was great and good. I dimly caught the notion of the martyred President as the standard bearer to the conscience of his countrymen, as the eagle had been the ensign of courage to the soldiers of the Wisconsin regiment."

Tragedy marked the end of Old Abe's turbulent career. He died in March, 1881, from suffocation caused by a fire that had originated in a pile of waste paper and other refuse. His remains were artistically stuffed and mounted, and for many years occupied a place of honor among the flags and souvenirs of war displayed in the rotunda of the Capitol. In the fire that destroyed the building in 1904 Old Abe went aloft in the flames. Nor was that the last fire to pursue him.

The hundred-thousand-dollar monument to Wisconsin's sol-

local demand. In the spring the owners of maple groves tried to supplement the output of sorghum by making maple syrup and maple sugar, but that also proved to be too expensive to compete with sugar imported into the state.

Finally in World War II the scarcity of labor reduced both the sorghum and the maple sugar industry to production for the local and luxury trade. Of the fifty-three million pounds of sweets produced in Wisconsin in 1945, sorghum and maple sugar constituted less than two per cent. About seventy-two per cent was beet sugar and some twenty-six per cent was honey. The products which furnished our forefathers with the ingredients for their candy and the syrup for their buckwheat cakes are dwindling from year to year. Only the honey bees have been able to edge forward.

My historical reverie came to a sudden end with a veer of the wind and the sight of another puff of vapor issuing from the cupola of the mill. Nestled in a roadside nook, against one of those steep hills peculiar to the landscape of central Sauk County, the weather-beaten sorghum mill of the Lohrs seemed to be sunning itself in the golden light of antiquity. For more than fifty years the elder Lohr and then his sons have pressed the sorghum cane grown by neighboring farmers and cooked the extracted juice into syrup. They use a recipe known only to the family and some of their German kinsfolk.

Farmers stacking their cane bundles in crisscross fashion explained to me some of the methods of cultivation. The soil must be rich and well prepared. Seeding is much the same as for corn, the rows being the same distance apart, and the crop is similarly cultivated except that it is often necessary to hoe the plants at least once to thin out an excessive number of stalks and to keep the weeds under control. The harvesting of sorghum,

sorghum

however, requires more hand labor than corn does. First the leaves are removed, usually by knocking them off with rapid strokes of a lath. Then the plumelike seed tops are denuded and the naked stalks are cut, tied into bundles, and hauled to the mill, where the juice is pressed out.

I stood for a time watching the cooking operations. A pungent smell filled the air. And the golden syrup itself was like distilled sunshine as it came from the vats. At the first break in the routine Herman Lohr paused to answer my questions.

"The canes are crushed by rollers operated by tractor power," he explained. "The process of making sorghum has changed little since the growing of sugar cane became popular during the Civil War days of sugar shortage. At one time Wisconsin was the leading sorghum-growing state in the Northwest, and there were conventions and a monthly journal to promote the industry.

"The most important factor is the soil. When I'm tending the pans in which the strained juice is being boiled down, I can tell from the evaporating steam on what kind of earth the crop has been grown, what kind of fertilizer has been used, and whether the crop has been well cultivated. For best results the field must be well prepared and free of weeds. Fifty years' experience in our family has taught us some of these simple facts.

"Our recipe for turning the juice into syrup is different from that in common use. To purify the juice we use a clay that is found in only a few places in this vicinity."

"Is not the clay to be found elsewhere?" I interposed, realizing that this was one of the secrets of producing the bland, light-colored syrup.

"I know of only one remaining pocket of that clay," Mr. Lohr told me. "When that is gone I don't know where another supply can be found in these hills."

Consulting some faded booklets on his desk, he gave me figures on the manufacture of sorghum syrup in Wisconsin. Whereas production had mounted from 19,854 gallons in 1859 to an all-time high of 314,150 gallons twenty years later, it has steadily declined since that time except for a brief period during World War I. In 1945, when the labor supply was so greatly depleted, the output declined to about 75,000 gallons. Most of the sorghum produced in Wisconsin is grown, processed, and sold in the southwestern part of the state. The per-acre yield of green material is from eight to fifteen tons, which will produce from 70 to 150 gallons of syrup. In 1945 the Office of Price Administration fixed the ceiling price at $2.25 a gallon.

"The methods used in the boiling and cooking of the juice determine the color and the flavor of the sorghum syrup," I was told by another miller, F. G. Lehman, who operates the cane mill near Watertown which his father started more than eighty years ago. "The old way of using clay as a purifier is out of date in this part of the state. Our method is to cook with gas and skim until the syrup is clear; personal attention is required. Sorghum, which was a standby in most pioneer Wisconsin families, is still in rural communities the surest and cheapest source of sweetening. Our neighbors, like ourselves, have it on the table at every meal. It saves sugar in these days of wartime shortages."

I visited some of the other mills in southern Wisconsin. At Rome and Waterford are the two factories operated by the second generation of the Reich family. Near Union Center is the mill of the Markee family, which has a secret method of finishing the syrup that attracts many customers. Not everyone can make good sorghum. It is a trade that requires long years of apprenticeship. The hours are long and the work laborious. Most of the sons of the old-time sorghum makers have refused to carry on, and many communities that once produced thousands of gallons each year—such as Rockdale, Sun Prairie, Rush Lake, and Westfield—have entirely suspended operations. Whereas Wisconsin once had over two hundred mills, there are today fewer than seventy-five.

But to the old-timers sorghum calls up many pleasant memories: pancakes with sorghum, fresh bread with sorghum, molasses candy. Small wonder they talk of the good old days.

Some people object to the tart taste of sorghum, but those who like it insist that homemade buckwheat cakes smothered in sorghum have no equal as a breakfast dish. Confessing my hunger for these old-fashioned breakfast cakes, I questioned many members of the older families about the recipe for them. Not one seemed to have it. I recalled that my mother began with what she called "spook yeast." She set a crock of it, wrapped in a blanket, on the warming oven at the first breath of cold weather. Each morning she reserved some part of the mixture as a starter for the next morning's batter.

I also questioned a number of retired salesmen, who seemed agreed that the Cole Hotel at Cashton in Monroe County almost always served breakfast cakes made the old way. I appealed to Mrs. Odelia Cole, retired head of the dining room, and from her got the recipe which had been used in her family for more than three quarters of a century:

Warm a pint of sweet milk and a pint of water. Put half this mixture in a stone crock, add five teacupfuls of buckwheat flour, and beat until smooth. Last add the rest of the milk and water and a teacupful of yeast.

Where you hold some yeast over each time, a tablespoonful of butter may be added in place of the milk. A beaten egg may also be added.

"Men who like good things to eat, served the old way, have three hungers," observed Mrs. Cole. "They hunger in the morning for buckwheat cakes spread with sorghum; at noon they want johnnycake and maple syrup; and at night they ask for baking-powder biscuits dripping with honey."

Determined that all three hungers should be satisfied, I awaited the arrival of the seasons. I had already visited the sorghum mills in the fall. In the spring I would visit the maple-sugar bushes. Come summer I would make tours of bee farms, large and small. I looked forward to the culinary delights that make men talk of mother's cooking.

March was ushered in with a storm, and for two days the snow hung heavy on the trees. When the thaw came with a changing wind, the clotted masses fell from the branches and splashed upon the ground below. The air cleared and the sun mounted; water overran the roads. Spring was in the air. But the robins seemed to delay. That night the roads were again frozen and a heavy frost coated the buildings.

The morning mail brought me an invitation from Everett Martin of Mukwonago, dean of the state's maple-syrup makers and owner of the largest maple grove in southern Wisconsin. He had tapped five hundred trees in the bush. Some were only fifty years old, others one hundred and fifty. His sixty-ninth season as a maker of maple syrup had begun.

He suggested that I come when syrup making would be at its best. "To produce a flow of sap," he wrote, "we must have alternate freezing—first frost and a few degrees below the freezing point at night. Up the next day to 40–45 degrees. The sap will flow for about thirty-six hours after the frost and then cease until another freeze. You will have to judge the time for your visit by the weather conditions."

For several days we had rain and fog, and I waited. Then one evening the sun reddened the horizon before it sank, and by morning a white frost had coated the outdoor world like a glazed doughnut. I was off.

When I entered the syrup house, Everett Martin, aged and bent from hard work, was busy skimming the froth off the pans of boiling sap. He came to greet me and talked a minute before he turned to poke up the fire. His momentary preoccupation gave me my opportunity to look about.

The building, standing beside the highway on a hill, consisted of two rooms. Large cylindrical galvanized vats of forty-barrel capacity occupy one room, the boiling outfit the other. After the raw sap is gathered in the woods by team it is piped from the tank wagons to storage, whence it flows by gravity through pipes to the boiling pans.

"That boiling pan was made at Bellows Falls, Vermont," said Mr. Martin, continuing the conversation. "It is fourteen feet long and over three feet wide, and is made up of twenty-five compartments with openings from one to the other so that the cooking sap must flow eighty-four feet before it stops at the far end. Every hour forty gallons of sap enters the upper end to be evaporated in that time to one gallon of maple syrup. A sugar-testing thermometer tells me when the syrup is ready to be withdrawn."

"Is there any special secret in the making of the syrup?" I asked as I tasted a sample in the steam-clouded room.

"None except the cooking: keeping the heat up and even, and the sap boiling so that the syrup will not scorch. As the hot syrup is withdrawn it is filtered through felt to remove the lime such as is found in ordinary drinking water. Lime gives syrup a dark color. The filterer purifies it and gives it a light-brown finish.

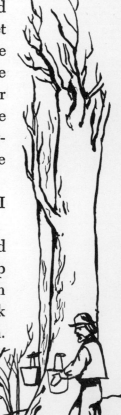

Every morning the boiling pans must be scoured to remove the lime just as from time to time lime must be removed from a teakettle. A lot of things can be done to spoil the syrup but nothing to improve it."

Twice a day when the sap run is at its height the tree buckets are emptied and the sap hauled in. So long as there is still sap in storage the cooking must go on. Sometimes it is a day-and-night job.

"Does it injure the trees to tap them every year?" I inquired.

"Does a mosquito that bites you for blood injure your health?" Mr. Martin asked facetiously. "It's about the same with the tapping of the maple tree for sap."

Because of the vast amount of work and the great expense that go into the making of maple syrup, profits are small and production is declining. Most of the syrup bushes in southern Wisconsin were discontinued years ago and the trees turned into fine flooring. But there are still many syrup makers who feel they cannot conscientiously retire, having worked at their trade so long. Others keep at it in the face of high costs because it has been a family tradition. The largest supply comes from Granton, Loyal, and Neillsville in Clark County; Antigo, Phlox, and Polar in Langlade County; Bowler, Mattoon, and Regina in Shawano County; Marathon and Wausau in Marathon County; Ellsworth and Plum City in Pierce County; and numerous other places in the central part of the state.

Before departing from Everett Martin's maple syrup house I observed him planing a short piece of lumber, the size of other board ends hanging on the wall. "These are my annual figures on syrup making," he explained, pointing to seasoned slabs on which he had recorded daily production figures. "We have five times as many orders on hand as we'll be able to fill," he grumbled, turning away once more to skim the sap boiling in the vat.

Honey production, though it is a younger industry in Wisconsin than the manufacture of maple sugar and sorghum, is commercially of greater importance. The father of beekeeping in Wisconsin is said to be Adam Grimm, a Bavarian immigrant who settled in Jefferson in 1849. He started experimenting with the black native bees, but found them lazy and vicious. Learning of a species of Italian bees that were said to be phenomenal honey-producers, he made a trip abroad and returned with a number of Italian queen bees. He became one of the first to make beekeeping a successful commercial enterprise. "I have more slaves working for me than all the slaveholders of the South ever dreamed of," he would playfully boast as he went among his two thousand colonies. "And my slaves," he would add with a twinkle in his eye, "are willing slaves."

The Italian strain of bees, distinguished by their yellow abdominal stripes, are easy to handle. More than five hundred colonies of them are owned by some ten or twelve apiarists in Wisconsin, notably at Ripon, Prairie du Sac, Menomonee Falls, Stanley, Loganville, Plain, Green Bay, Menomonie, and Ladysmith. From twelve to eighteen thousand farmers in the state each have a few swarms, from which they obtain enough honey for their own and their neighbors' use. Among the beekeepers I visited was Daniel Ott of Sauk City, who has eighty colonies on a cliff above the Wisconsin River. Out of the solid rock two rooms have been hewn in which Mr. Ott extracts his honey and stores his bees in winter.

Bees do more than make honey. Most of the fruit trees, wild plants, and field crops like alfalfa depend on fertilization by insects, and bees are the most numerous pollinators. Wisconsin's reputation as a "beekeepers' paradise," an epithet at least fifty years old, is attributed to the abundance of honey-producing plants that grow in the state.

For a long time Wisconsin has been producing more honey than is needed for local consumption, and it has become an important article of trade. In most years Wisconsin ranks from third to eighth among the honey-producing states, with a yield ranging from ten to thirty million pounds. For the commercial market the State Department of Agriculture has set up standard grades. About eighty-five per cent of the total product is extracted, much of this being consumed in the baking trade. Most of the balance is sold as comb.

old-fashion beehive

In almost every community where bees are raised dwells at least one man who is part spy, part naturalist. He pursues his vocation only in the fall after the frost has nipped and blackened the last wild flower. He is a "bee hunter," and his job is to locate the swarms of bees that have escaped from their owners during the summer and rob them of the honey they have stored for the winter. To trap the fugitives into revealing their clandestine home in the hollow of some tree tests his knowledge of the bee's habits and his own ingenuity.

The octogenarian William M. Neefe, last of the famous bee hunters of Richland County, told me of some of the artifices he had used to capture more than a hundred swarms. "After a shallow box, well scented with anise oil and containing a bit of honey, has been placed on a stump," he explained, "the bee hunter builds a little fire of twigs and sticks so arranged that the smoke will carry toward the forest." He gathered a few chips and pieces of wood to show how small the blaze must be. "When the fire has turned to embers, bits of honeycomb, the older and blacker the better, are then laid on the coals. This makes a dark smudge. In a few minutes the first bee will arrive, following close to the ground in the smoke.

"That explorer will dart around a bit before alighting and entering the box to gorge. Other bees follow, using the same tactics. As each bee leaves the box it rises high and circles around three or four times to get directions and landmarks that will enable it to find the spot again. After a few trips it is able to make a 'beeline' for home. Soon the box will be black with bees.

"To determine the distance of the tree in which the bees have lodged, one of them is sprinkled with flour and the time required to make the round trip is noted. Sometimes a second fire is started some distance away and a cross 'beeline' established. These lines will lead unerringly to the bee tree."

"Once within the forest, is it easy to locate the tree?" I inquired.

"That's the catch," the old bee hunter replied. Walking over to an elm tree, he pointed out knots and broken branches that would have to be examined as possible entrance ways. "There were times," he said, "when I found that the bees dropped down from the treetops to the ground and entered their home through a root; or it may have been a place where the trees had split or a branch had been broken off. Sometimes I had to lie on the ground until I saw them arriving in the sunlight or I had to locate them by sound. I never gave up until I found them. Then I cut my initials on the opposite side of the tree to establish my ownership."

beekeepers' garb

Toward the end of his recital of the arts of the bee detective Mr. Neefe returned to his place on the box. The years seemed to fall away, and he reached out his hand as if to pick up the ax. "All that remains," he concluded, "is to cut the tree, keep the bees down with ordinary wood smoke, and remove the honey.

If the bees are also wanted, the task after that is a simple one for the beekeeper."

"And the honey! How much would you ordinarily get from your raid?"

"If it was a young swarm, only a pailful or less. From an old swarm I have taken as much as two washtubs piled high."

"Bee hunting has lost much of its attractiveness with the cutting off of so many forests," reminisced the old man as he returned to the house to sit again beside the warm March fire. "But as long as there are bees some swarms will get away, and I hope there will always be men like myself who will see real sport in finding them. If my sight and hearing were only better, I would rather play hooky hunting bees this spring than work in my garden."

When Wisconsin was a land of forests there were many such bee hunters. They were pointed out in their communities, and still are, just as the good fox or deer hunter is today. Among them were Charles Giaugue of Stanley, Newell France of Platteville, Fred Mook of Lancaster, Ira Andes of Cassville, Clifford Wood of South Wayne, Kermit Johnson of Wild Rose, Frank Dilts of Wautoma, Albert Smith of Waupaca, Fred Hoff of Redgranite, John Atkins of Almond, and George Zick and Henry Mettel of Prairie du Sac.

In 1922 a library on beekeeping was established at the University's College of Agriculture in memory of America's great beekeeper Charles C. Miller of Marengo, Illinois. In that collection, the world's largest on the subject, are more than five thousand books and journals in all languages, the oldest of which dates back to 1590, and a number of priceless manuscripts. It is a "golden treasury" which is consulted by men from all parts of the world.

Christmas in Wisconsin: Yuletide Customs Old and New

IN WISCONSIN THE OBSERVANCE OF THE YULETIDE RUNS THE gamut of customs dear to the nations of Christendom. The Yankees of the south-central part of the state clothe the Christmas season with solemnity and dignity. In many communities Old World traditions hallowed by the centuries continue to be faithfully observed: special culinary treats, singing and games appropriate to the season, religious rites, and different forms of the Santa Claus legend. In some of them the season extends from St. Nicholas Day, December 6, to Twelfth Night, January 6. In others it is even longer.

"In our family," I have been told by a neighbor of Dutch ancestry, "there were always two Christmas celebrations, a custom my grandfather brought with him from Holland. My own

105

father, whose name was Nicholas, never let the family forget St. Nicholas Day. The grandchildren, too, came to know St. Nicholas Day, but the family now has the standard one-celebration Christmas." Go where you will, however, you will discover that outside the big cities the German- and Dutch-settled communities still observe St. Nicholas Day.

About the time others are bringing their festivities to a close the Russians are just beginning theirs. The reason is that the Orthodox Church uses the Julian rather than the Gregorian calendar, which differs by thirteen days. The Epiphany, or "Little Christmas," in the Western World's calendar is the date set in the Russian calendar for the commemoration of the Savior's birth. Some nationalities carry the Christmas celebration along until Ash Wednesday, when it is abruptly terminated by the opening of Lent. The Czechs at Yuba in Richland County, for instance, participate in a two-day pre-Lenten dance.

The depth and sincerity of the Christmas spirit among Wisconsin people may perhaps be attributed largely to their Old World ancestry. Their customs vary with nationality, creed, and community. Santa Claus is Holland's St. Nicholas. The Christmas tree originated in Germany, the candles in France, the wreaths in Italy, the Christmas card in England, and the outdoor decorations on our own North American continent.

Even the Christmas meal is usually an index to the family's nationality. The Germans have their *Stollen,* made in wreaths, braids, and other designs, to eat for the holiday breakfast and *Pfeffernuesse* to nibble on between meals. The Moravians have their gingerbread, the Bulgarians their punch, the Czechs their lamb cake, the Irish their Tom and Jerry, the Welsh their special holiday bread, *bara ceirich,* the Cornish their saffron cake, and the Norwegians their *øl,* a mild ale made from hops. A visit to

grandmother's for Christmas dinner is still the event of the day in many families.

Somewhat less popular today than a half century ago is the old-time English plum pudding. A gala sight it was when it was brought to the table all ablaze, scenting the air with its spicy aroma. But its preparation required days of work, and today, when one may buy an acceptable substitute at the bakery, the old custom is observed only in families where help is available or the housewife herself has time and enthusiasm for holiday baking. In its place a fruit cake or rich mince pie is served.

Roast goose, too, immortalized by Dickens' Tiny Tim, has almost disappeared from the present-day menu. Until fairly recently it was as much the *pièce de résistance* of the Christmas dinner as was turkey of the Thanksgiving feast. The large amount of fat the goose contains is less palatable to the present-day taste than it was to an older generation's. In an occasional community, however, it still occupies a place on the menu. In Watertown, for instance, goose continues to appear on the hotel bills of fare the year round.

The use of evergreens for decorations was a natural development in Wisconsin, where the whole Northland was an evergreen forest. In Protestant communities the evergreen tree is the usual decoration not only for the home but also for the pulpit and chancel of the church, a custom said to have originated with Martin Luther himself. Approximately a million trees, estimates Mr. C. L. Harringtcn, director of the Forest and Parks Division of the Wisconsin Conservation Department, are used each year in the homes of the state. These are chiefly spruce and balsam, produced in northern Wisconsin, and Douglas fir, which is shipped in from the West. "The use of trees of relatively small size such as the Christmas tree," Mr. Harrington observes, "affords an outlet for a practical and sustaining forestry operation."

Folk customs of one sort and another are still to be observed in many scattered communities. Among people of Swedish ancestry in Polk County a sheaf of grain is put out for the birds. In many homes a candle is left burning at the window throughout the night as an invitation to the Christ child. In some households of English ancestry the father, at the close of the Christmas dinner, partly fills a large platter with raisins and drenches them with brandy. These are then lighted and each member of the family is invited to claim his portion.

Families of Yugoslavian extraction bake a Christmas cake in which is hidden a coin that will bring good luck to the person whose slice contains it. About Viroqua masked Norwegian carolers visit the farmers of the neighborhood and entertain them with antics and song until their identity is guessed.

The Finnish people gather on New Year's Eve to cast their fortunes for the coming year. This is done by pouring some molten substance into a bucketful of cold water. In the early days it was usually pitch from the pine tree, later tin or lead. As the substance congeals it assumes, with the aid of the participants' imagination, the shape of some article that symbolizes the future. If, for instance, it resembles a flower, marriage is in the offing; if a boat, a voyage; if a coin, riches; if a rod, poverty. Whatever it was, the owner would save it as a token of the future in store for him.

Modern innovations are the splendid outdoor displays that have become so general and the huge community Christmas trees ablaze with electrically lighted candles. The cities of northern Wisconsin vie with one another to produce the most beautiful pine-tree display. In Marshfield, which is probably deserving of top honors, the long, wide boulevard stretching across the city is lighted and spanned with evergreen arches at Christmastime. A truly beautiful sight it is.

In years when the weather has been favorable the town of Waupun has put on an exhibit of snow sculpturing that has inspired great wonder and admiration. When the snow has been wet enough to roll, snow figures of the Nativity scene, both human and animal, have been modeled and arranged in the yards of the Lutheran churches. On two occasions during a winter of the first World War I saw in a dooryard a sculptured madonna bowed in prayer. Both times I stopped my car to join in the meditation. To me she suggested a virgin clothed in the white garments of heaven, beseeching God to grant her wish. Her head was tilted heavenward as if to let Him see how earnestly she made her supplication. Perhaps, I thought, she was praying for the return of some devotee serving his country. Perhaps the candle she held was a beacon to guide his steps aright.

In 1913 Milwaukee had the first of the community Christmas trees and celebrations that have since become a regular part of the city's activities. Every year since then except those of World War II, when sign-lighting was restricted, a Christmas Eve program has been given, in which public employees play an important part. During three of the war years the Milwaukee Archdiocesan Council of Catholic Women staged in place of a lighted tree the Bethlehem manger scene, with life-size figures of Mary and Joseph and the arrival of the Three Wise Men. After 1945, when the community tree was resumed, the crèche was given a place on the lawn of the old Court House near St. John's Cathedral. At both places thousands have gathered when Christmas events have been announced.

In the early days, of course, Christmas celebrations revolved entirely about the home and the church. For the children in German and Dutch communities St. Nicholas Day was a minor Christmas celebration. "They received nuts, candy, and fruit but nothing more substantial," my Dutch-descended neighbor has told me. "St. Nick functioned as did Santa Claus later in the month. A noise at the door and there he was. Only we could never quite glimpse either him or Santa Claus. On Christmas Day we got, besides such edibles as came to us on St. Nicholas Day, such presents as wearing apparel, none too enthusiastically received at that age, and shiny toys that were more exciting."

To impress the children St. Nicholas was generally employed as a forerunner of Santa Claus, who made inquiries about each child—his conduct and his desires. Did the youngsters help with the chores, bring in the wood and water, say their prayers? Communities which did not observe St. Nicholas Day employed a similar device. Santa Claus's wife would arrive early on Christmas Eve to put the same questions. Stick in hand, dressed in white robes, she would demand affirmative replies from the parents while the children stood by speechless with wonder and trembling with excitement.

"The Santa Claus Lady," wrote a participant in such an event three-quarters of a century later, "gave us a few nuts and a stick of horehound candy, or a few peppermint balls, saying that she would speak in our behalf to Santa Claus and tell him what good children we had been and that he must try to come to our house and bring us a few things. She told us not to count too much on his coming as he was very busy and might not be able to get to our house as it was rather far in the country. We were filled with uncertainty, but he never failed us."

The custom of exchanging gifts with family and friends at Christmastide is an ancient one dating from the Three Wise

Men, who brought to the infant Jesus gold and frankincense and myrrh. But it was not at this season that gifts were distributed in the early French settlements. "Christmas was not the day to give and receive presents," wrote the widow of Green Bay's distinguished lawyer Henry S. Baird in later years; "this was reserved for New Year's." New Year's rather than Christmas was also the time for the singing of carols. Gradually the customs shifted until today the exchange of gifts and the singing of carols have become features of Christmas celebrations everywhere.

In these earlier days it was considered bad taste in many communities to present a gift that had not been made with one's own hands. Throughout the fall mothers and grandmothers spent long evenings knitting socks, mittens, and other garments. The menfolk made sleds, bending hickory staves into curved runners; wooden skates with steel-surfaced runners; wooden tops that could be spun with a cord; and doll furniture.

Most of the early dolls were made of cornhusks, rags, knitted yarn, or wood. They were none too lifelike until papier-mâché began to be used for the heads and wax for the faces. Many of the first commercially manufactured dolls were French ladies illustrating the latest fashion modes. Of these fashionable ladies Mrs. Alice Trimpey of Baraboo assembled what is probably the largest collection in the state. It rivals that of the late Mrs. Theodore Roosevelt.

In this twentieth century the vogue has been for dolls that are realistic reproductions of the small child: the "character" dolls that appeared in 1910, the Bye-Lo Baby of the early twenties, the Dy-Dee Doll of a somewhat later day, and many others. Every Christmas has brought new doll creations to gladden the hearts of countless children.

But the child on the frontier knew nothing of these. Nor was its Christmas any less wonderful on that account than the modern child's. From an eighty-two-year-old correspondent in Baraboo I have recently had a letter in which she records her vivid memories of childhood Christmases in Wisconsin:

"The things I remember are not unusual. Mother strung a long rope across the living room, on which we all hung our stockings. We had a Christmas tree also. We were sent upstairs early, but went down quietly on the stairs and tried to peep at them as they put up the presents.

"Next morning an orange in one's stocking, along with candy and popcorn, was the greatest treat. For with no fruit stores as we now have them, oranges were to be found in the stores only at Christmastime. An orange for Christmas! That was something to remember and feel proud of having received! It was something worth telling to your playmates.

"Christmas Eve services were held in the old Methodist church, and when we were older we were allowed to go along. I recall that inside the edifice were two long stoves—one on each side—filled with burning cordwood, from which ran stovepipes the full length of the church. Suspended by wires from the ceiling under the stovepipe joints were quart tin pails to catch the liquid soot that dripped. Light thrown into the church by silvered reflectors fastened to the wall behind the kerosene lamps gave all the light that was needed.

"At the front of the church stood a large candlelighted Christmas tree for the Sunday School, but it was loaded with presents for the grownups as well. When the program carols had been sung the presents were distributed. Popcorn and candy were given out to the congregation, and the older children scrambled to capture the loops of popcorn and apples that decorated the tree.

"In those days everybody came to the church festivities in horse-drawn bobsleighs. With straw in the bottom of the sleigh box, soapstones at our feet, and covered with buffalo robes, we were kept warm for the ride. During the exercises the horses were heavily blanketed; at the end they were frisky as they sensed the imminence of the trip back to the farm barn."

With slight variations, perhaps, that was the Christmas scene in many a Wisconsin home before the advent of the twentieth century. And it is not too different today except for the inevitable changes wrought by modernity: Santa Claus's multiple appearances on the streets to chat with the children; their suppliant letters to him at his Northern abode; and the radio stories which throw them into such a state of excitement that they start counting the seemingly endless days which must elapse before Santa will arrive to fill their stockings and decorate the tree.

As the shadows close in on the night before Christmas the preparations that have been going forward for months finally cease. Every member of the family smiles with happiness. The younger children, petulant from endless waiting, are hurried off to bed with the promise that they will be called early next morning. After the Christmas tree is hung with glittering ornaments the family prepares for the church services. The Protestant churches give programs in which the Sunday School children participate. Catholic families await the hour for the midnight mass.

The midnight mass, now so well established among Roman Catholics, was introduced slowly. Midnight masses had, it is true, been celebrated annually at the Capuchin monastery founded in 1857 at Mount Calvary in Fond du Lac County and in the churches established by the order in Wisconsin. Nevertheless its general introduction was opposed by many Catholic editors, priests, and prelates. There were those who feared that

pre-holiday revelers might disturb the worshipers; that the very novelty of the innovation might inspire irreverence and mar the solemnity of the anniversary rites. Others felt that it was more fitting for fathers and mothers to accompany their children to communion on Christmas morning. One Catholic editor wrote that he believed the midnight mass should be celebrated only once every hundred years, to inaugurate the new century and commemorate the one that was passing.

After 1900, however, the midnight mass gained ground steadily. On December 22, 1906, the *Catholic Citizen* of Milwaukee announced, with some misgivings perhaps, that "an unusual number of churches will revive the custom of having midnight mass. A few years ago this custom was confined to St. Francis church, but this year several of the churches will usher in Christmas with solemn high mass." Within a few years the clergy generally had accepted the idea of the midnight mass. It has had a great appeal to worshipers, who crowd the churches to participate in this service. The special music, the choral singing, and the hushed solemnity of the ritual kindle the imagination and sense of the mystical. A great many of the attendants at Christmas Eve masses are not regular churchgoers.

In churches of all denominations, especially in the cities, Christmas Eve and Christmas Day services are marked by the singing of carols and hymns, many of which are centuries old. They never lose their appeal. One day some weeks before Christmas a neighbor and I were sauntering along talking of olden days and half listening to music that was being broadcast from atop the buildings on the Capitol Square in Madison. Gradually the surroundings seemed to fade. Oblivious of the crowds surging about us, we stood silent on the street corner, enraptured by a voice singing the hymn of the ages:

Joy to the world! the Lord is come!
Let earth receive her King;
Let every heart prepare him room,
And heaven and nature sing.

It was a Christmas concert on the air, the first to which I had listened. My Christmas began then and there as I listened to the messages of joy and good will that rang out into the night: *Adeste Fideles; Hark! the Herald Angels Sing; O Little Town of Bethlehem; We Three Kings of Orient Are; While Shepherds Watched Their Flocks*—songs of devotion for all believers. Then the music stopped. Again we were surrounded by hurrying shoppers, and I came back to the bustling workaday present.

Of all the childhood experiences my old friends have recalled for me from time to time, one in particular seems to be vividly stamped upon their memories: the return home at Christmastime after a more or less extended absence. Always the narrator dwells upon the nostalgic emotions awakened by the homeward drive through the winter countryside. The snow-rutted roads had been coated with sheen by the runners of cutters and sleighs that had borne others home for a reunion with families and neighbors. Lights gleamed from every farm home, casting myriad shadows across the white coverlet of snow. What can be more beautiful than contoured mounds of fresh deep snow under the moon's silvery light? Who is not stirred by the memory of the crisp winter air spangled with sparkling frost; the moon gliding above the hills to the occasional thunder of frost-riven trees; the tinkling sounds carried by the breezes of the night; the even breathing of the belled horses?

At last the traveler stops. A door opens. Mother! Dad! For the moment all cares, all sorrows vanish. The spirit of peace rules the earth.

INDEX

Abraham Lincoln Road, 34

Addams, Jane, visits "Old Abe," 90

Ale, manufacture of, 64

Andes, Ira, bee hunter, 104

Anemone, 4, 5

Antigo, syrup production in, 100

Appleton, railroad to, 36

Arbutus, 6, 11, 12

Architecture, early, 15-22, 61-62

Arrowhead, habitat of, 8

Arctic primrose, 5

Asters, 3, 7, 12

Astor, John Jacob, 17

Atkins, John, bee hunter, 104

Automobiles, 39-42

Babcock, Stephen M., 12

Bach, Christopher, 69

Bachelor's-button, 12

Baileys Harbor, flora at, 5

Baird, Henry S., 30

Baird, Mrs. Henry S., quoted, 111

Ballard, A. W., automobile of, 40

Baraboo, 11, 24

Barbershops, early, 51-55

Barnes Prairie, 11

Barnum, P. T., 89

Bear Creek, 46, 48

Becker, William, 53

Beekeeping, 101-104

Beer, use and manufacture of, 63-64; price, 67. *See also* Saloons

Beer gardens, 67-69

Belgians, houses of, 22

Belleville, early store near, 60

Belmont, territorial capital, 19, 30

Belmont Mound, 30

Beloit, cobblestone houses at, 21

Berners, Edward C., 77-78

Bicycles, 38-39

Big Bend, 34

Bittersweet, 12

Black-eyed Susan, 11

Black Hawk Slough, 7

Black Hawk War, 31

Blatz, Valentin, brewer, 65

Bloodroot, habitats of, 4, 5

Blue Mounds, early landmark, 28-29, 30; television towers on, 43

Boscobel, bridge at, 35

Bowler, syrup making at, 100

Bridgeport, bridge at, 35

Bridges, 35

Brisbois, Michael, house of, 17, 24

Brodhead, bridge at, 35

Burlington, old architecture at, 21

Busch's, Milwaukee saloon, 72

Bush clover, 11

Cabinetmaking, 25

Cactus, 9-10

Cactus Bluff, 9-10

Cambridge, flora at, 8

Camp Randall, 87, 92

Canada mayflower, 8

Canals, 32

Canoe travel, 29, 30

Capuchin monastery, 113

Carhart, J. W., invents automobile, 39

Cedar Creek, bridge spanning, 35

Cedarburg, bridge at, 35

Chicago, Milwaukee and St. Paul Railway, 36

Christmas, length of season, 105-106; folk customs, 106, 107-108; food for, 106-107; decorations, 107, 108-109; pioneer celebrations, 109-113; modern, 113-114

Churches, Christmas services of, 112, 113-114

Clarence Crossing, bridge at, 35

Clothing, *see* Dress

Cobban, Alexander J., 41

Cornishmen, houses of, 19, 24

Corsets, crusade against, 44-50

Crabapple, wild, 4

Creatore, Giuseppe, band leader, 69

Curtin, Jeremiah, birthplace of, 24

Curtis, John T., 13

Czechs, Christmas custom of, 106

Daggett, Henry L., anti-lacing crusade of, 46-50

Davis, J. J., 11

Decoration Day, 4

Dekorra, road to, 32

De Soto, flora at, 7

Deutsches Dorf, Watertown inn, 75

Devil's Lake State Park, ferns at, 8

Dilts, Frank, bee hunter, 104

Dodge, Governor Henry, 19

Dodgeville, flora at, 6

Dodgeville Hotel, 34

Dogwood, 8

Dolls, 111

Door County, flora of, 4-5; architecture of Belgians in, 22

Doorways, 23-24

Dorner, Otto, 38

Dornfeld, Paul, barber, 52-54

Doty, James D., 19, 30

Dousman, Hercules L., house of, 17

Dress, for automobiling, 42; footwear, 60-61. *See also* Corsets

Dubuque, road terminal, 31

Dunkel Inn, 33

Dunn, Judge Charles, 19

Duryea automobile, 40

Dutch, Christmas customs of, 105-106, 110

Dutchman's-breeches, 4, 5

Eau Claire, 45, 47, 87

Eel Pot Club, 55

Egg House, Milwaukee saloon, 72

Elkhorn, old architecture at, 20

Ellsworth, syrup making at, 100

Farmhouses, architecture of, 21-23

Faville, Stoughton W., conservationist, 13; home of, 24-25

Faville Prairie Preserve, 13-14

Fennimore, railroad to, 36

Ferns, habitats of, 8

Finns, houses of, 22; Christmas customs of, 108

Fireplaces, 24-25

Flora of Wisconsin, 3-14; and pioneer customs, 4; legal protection of, 12-14

Fond du Lac, 48; old architecture at, 20; road to, 32; railroad to, 36

Food, sale of, 56, 57; served in hotels, 59; in saloons, 66, 67, 72-73, 74; sugar and syrups, 93-102; for Christmas, 106-107

Fort Atkinson, old architecture at, 20

Fort Crawford, built, 30; road to, 31

Fort Howard, built, 30; road to, 31. *See also* Green Bay

Fort Wilkins, road terminal, 34

Fort Winnebago, built, 30

Fowler, Orson S., 20

Fox Lake, town of, 32

Fox-Wisconsin waterway, 29, 30, 31, 32, 35

France, Newell, bee hunter, 104

Fredericks, Robert "Barney," 70

French, posts of, 29

Fringed gentian, 5

Fuller, Albert M., quoted, 5, 12

Furniture and household goods, 19, 23, 25, 26, 33

Gahlman, Garret M., 75
Gallagher, John, saloonkeeper, 70
Garden Club of America, 5
Genske, Fritz, saloonkeeper, 74
Gentians, 5, 13
Germans, and use of beer, 63-65; social life of, 66, 67; Christmas customs, 106, 109-110
Gettelman, Adam, 65
Giaugue, Charles, 104
Giffey, Charles W., 78
Gilbert, road to, 34
Ginger plant, 5
Golden glow, pioneer culture of, 12
Goldenrods, 3, 7
Goodrich, Joseph, hexagonal house of, 20
Granton, produces syrup, 100
Green Bay, 30; early houses at, 16-17, 20; French post, 29; road terminal, 31, 32, 34; railway terminal, 36; automobile race from, 39-40; beekeeping at, 101; marsh hay from, 82. *See also* Fort Howard
Greenbush, inn in, 34
Grignon, Charles A., house of, 17
Grimm, A. R., 53
Grimm, Adam, apiarist, 101
Guth, Alexander C., 15, 18

Hales Corners, 24
Hallauer, George, 77-78
Hamacher, John, saloon of, 74-75
Hanks, Lucien M., 80
Harper, Colonel John, 70
Hausmann's, Madison saloon, 74, 75
Haven, J. B., store, 58
Hawthorn bush, 4
Heiser's, *see* Mother Heiser's
Hepatica, 4
Hexagonal houses, 20

Highways, *see* Transportation
Hill, John F., 89
Historic American Buildings Survey, 15-16
Hoff, Fred, bee hunter, 104
Hollyhock, 12
Honey production, 101-102. *See also* Beekeeping
Hope Lake Bog, flora in, 8-9
Horicon, 20, 82
Horlick, William, 79
Horses, *see* Transportation
Horseshoe Lake, flora at, 7
Hotchkiss, W. O., 41
Hotels and inns, 33-34, 57, 58-59; bars of, 72
Houses, pioneer, 15-27
Howe Brothers, Stoughton store, 56-57, 58
Hudson, old architecture at, 20
Hunt House, 21
Hustisford, barbershop at, 51-54
Hutson House, Stoughton hotel, 57

Ice cream sundae, invention of, 77-80
Ice harvesting industry, 81-85
Indians, highways of, 28-29, 30
Inns, *see* Hotels and inns
Interstate Park, ferns in, 8
Irish, Christmas drink of, 106
Isenring's Milwaukee resort, 72

Jack-in-the-pulpit, habitats of, 5, 6
Janesville, early road to, 32; railway point, 36
Jeche, Paul, 53
Jensen, Jens, 5
Jesse Smith Inn, 34
Johnson, Edward, 79
Johnson, Kermit, bee hunter, 104
Jolliet, Louis, 29

Kaukauna, Grignon house at, 17
Kenealy, Arabella, quoted, 45-46
Kienitz, John F., quoted, 20
Kirby Hotel (Milwaukee), 72
Kirchhayn, log house at, 21
Kleiner, Leo A., 56, 58, 59
Kuenstlerheim, Milwaukee saloon, 72

Lackner, Francis, 71
La Crosse, flora at, 7
Ladysmith, apiary at, 101
La Follette, Robert M., 58
Lake Geneva, source of ice, 83
Lake Katherine, source of ice, 83
Lake Mills, icehouses at, 83
Lake Monona, flora at, 5
Lake Park (Milwaukee), 72
Lake Puckaway, cacti at, 10
Lake Wingra, arboretum at, 13
Lake Winnebago, source of ice, 83
Lancaster, 58; old houses at, 18, 20
Lange, Louie A., 48
Langlade, Charles de, 17
Levitan, Solomon, quoted, 23
Lewis, Governor James T., 55
Lichtenberg, Fred, 53
Lilies, 3, 7, 11, 12
Little Norway, 22
Loganville, apiary at, 101
Lotus, 7, 12
Loyal, produces syrup, 100
Lucia Brothers, Green Bay firm, 40-41
Lueddemann's on the Lake, 72
Lueddemann's on the River, 72
Lupine, habitats of, 6

McCann, Daniel, 87
McKay, William J., 87
Madison, 58; arboretum at, 13; early road to, 31; railway to, 36; auto-mobile race to, 39; saloons at, 74-75; ice industry in, 83, 85
Mag Lawe, early inn, 34
Mail, transportation of, 32
Malted milk, invention of, 79
Maple syrup, making of, 98-101
Marathon, produces syrup, 100
Marquette, Jacques, 29
Marquette, village of, cacti at, 10
Marshfield, Christmas displays at, 108
Martin, Everett, house of, 21; syrup maker, 98-101
Martin, Morgan L., 30
Mattoon, syrup production in, 100
May Day, observance of, 4
Mayflower, habitat of, 8
Medicines, patent, 60
Memorial Day, 4
Menominee Indian Reservation, 34
Menomonee Falls, apiary at, 101
Menomonie, apiary at, 101
Mettel, Henry, bee hunter, 104
Michigan Territory, 30
Miller, Charles C., apiarist, 104
Milton, hexagonal house at, 20
Milwaukee, early roads to, 31, 32; railway terminal, 36; breweries and saloons, 64-73; ice industry in, 84; Christmas celebrations, 109
Milwaukee and Mississippi River Railway, 36
Milwaukee and Rock River Canal Company, 32
Milwaukee Garden, 67-68
Milwaukee River, canal project, 32; source of ice, 84
Milwaukee-Watertown Plank Road, 33
Mineral Point, old houses at, 18, 19-20
Mitchell, Reverend Samuel, 18

Mitchell-Rountree house, 18

Moccasin flower, habitat of, 8, 9

Monches, 82

Mook, Fred, bee hunter, 104

Moonlight Bay, flora at, 5

Moravians, Christmas food of, 106

Mormon houses, 21

Mosinee, flora at, 6

Mother Heiser's, Milwaukee saloon, 71

Mount Calvary, 113

Mount Horeb, Norwegian community at, 22; early road to, 31

Mount Vernon, 60

Muir, John, quoted, 7

Mukwonago, old house at, 21; syrup mill, 98-100

Muscoda, bridge at, 35

Music, in beer gardens and saloons, 69, 70, 75, 76. *See also* Songs and carols

Names, Christian, 26

Neefe, William M., bee hunter, 102-104

Neenah, old architecture at, 20

Neillsville, syrup production, 100

New Glarus, cacti at, 10

North Lake, source of ice, 83

North Western Railroad, 31, 36

Norwegians, architecture of, 22; Christmas customs, 106, 108

Octagonal houses, 20

Odell, Emery A., 41

Okauchee House, 34

Olbrich, Michael B., 13

"Old Abe," war eagle, 86-92

Old Agency House, 21

Old Military Road, 31

Ontonagon, 34

Orchids, 5, 12, 13

Oshkosh, railroad to, 36; automobile built in, 40

Ott, Daniel, apiarist, 101

Owens, Richard G., 64

Oyster Bar, Milwaukee saloon, 72

Pabst, Frederick, 65

Pabst Park (Shooting Park), 71

Pancake, Milwaukee saloon, 72

Pansy, culture of, 11

Pasqueflower, 4, 5, 7-8

Peat bogs, flora in, 8-9

Peck, Governor George W., 38

Pennington, E. J., 40

Peony, culture of, 12

Pewaukee, old architecture at, 20

Pewaukee Lake, source of ice, 83

Pfister Hotel (Milwaukee), 72

Phlox, syrup making at, 100

Pitcher plant, 8, 9, 11, 12

Plain, apiary at, 101

Plants of Wisconsin, 3-14

Platte Mound, early landmark, 30

Platteville, flora at, 6; rose culture, 12; old houses, 18-19

Platteville State Teachers College, 18

Pleasant Valley Park, Milwaukee beer garden, 72

Pleurisy root, 12

Plum City, syrup making at, 100

Polar, syrup making at, 100

Politics, discussions of, 51-62 *passim*

Porlier-Tank cottage, 16-17

Port Washington, *see* Sauk Harbor

Portage, 30. *See also* Fort Winnebago; Old Agency House

Post Road, 32

Potosi, 32

Prairie du Chien, flora at, 6, 7; old houses at, 17, 20, 24; French post,

29; territorial court, 30; early road to, 31. *See also* Fort Crawford
Prairie du Sac, apiary at, 101
Prien, John, store of, 55-56
Prospect Hill, old architecture at, 21
Pryor's Band, 69

Quentin's Park, *see* Schlitz Park
Quilts and quilting bees, 25

Racine, old architecture at, 21; road to, 31-32; automobiles built in, 39, 40; malted milk made in, 79-80
Railroads, *see* Transportation
Random Lake, source of ice, 83
Rawson, Captain M. J., 87
Regina, syrup making at, 100
Rexford, Eben E., flower grower, 11
Rhinelander, flora at, 6
Richards, John, house of, 20
Ridges Sanctuary, 5
Ridgeway, 34
Ripon, 25, 101
River travel, 29-30
Roads, *see* Transportation
Robert Dunkel Inn, 33
Robinson, Doane, 34
Rock Lake, source of ice, 83
Rockbridge, flora at, 6
Rocky Arbor Roadside Park, 8
Roi, Joseph, house of, 16
Roman Catholic Christmas, 113-114
Rood, Captain Hosea W., 87
Rose, David, Milwaukee mayor, 70
Rose, wild, 11; yellow, 12
Rosemary, habitat of, 8
Rosendale, peonies at, 12
Rountree, Major John H., 18
Ruggles Inn, 34
Rusk, Jeremiah, 33
Russians, Christmas of, 106

St. Croix Falls, cacti at, 10
Saloons, as social institution, 63-67, 73; in Milwaukee, 65-73; in northern Wisconsin, 73-74; in Madison, 74-75; at Watertown, 75
Sarau, Chris, 48
Sauerhering, Douglas L., 40
Sauk City, cacti at, 10; apiary, 101
Sauk County, hop production in, 64-65
Sauk Harbor (Port Washington), road terminal, 32
Schlitz, Joseph, brewer, 65
Schlitz Palm Garden, 66, 68-69
Schlitz Park (Quentin's Park), 66, 68
Schloemer, Gottfried, 40
Schuetzen (Shooting) Park, 71
Shaving mugs, 52-53
Sholes, Judge, saloon of, 71
Shooting star, habitats of, 6
Sinipee, road terminal, 32
Sinsinawa Mound, early landmark, 30
Sky, Chippewa chief, 87
Smith, Albert, bee hunter, 104
Smith, Denton J., store of, 60-62
Smith, Jesse, inn of, 34
Smith, Robert, 61
Soda fountains, 79
Songs and carols, 11, 26, 108, 114-115
Sorghum, making and use of, 93-97
Sperry, Theodore, cited, 14
Spiderwort, 3
Stagecoaches, 33, 51-52
Standard time, 36-37
Stanley, apiary at, 101
Stores, country, 52, 55-62. *See also* Barbershops
Stoughton, early hotel of, 57-58
Stumpner, Harry, cabinetmaker, 25
Sturgeon Bay, ice industry at, 83, 84
Swedes, Christmas customs, 108
Sweet william, 12

Tamarack bogs, flora of, 8
Terrace Garden, Milwaukee saloon, 71
Thomas, Theodore A., 69
Tobacco, use and sale of, 56, 57, 59-60
Toole, William, flower grower, 11
Trail trees, 29
Trailing arbutus, 6, 11, 12
Transportation: water highways, 29-30; horseback, 30; canals, 32; roads, 30-32, 33-35, 38, 41, 42; bridges, 35; railroad, 35-37; horse-drawn vehicles, 37-38, 113, 115; bicycles, 38-39; automobiles, 39-42
Trillium, 4, 6, 12
Tripp, Freeman L., 45
Turck, Christian, house of, 21
Turk's-cap lily, 3, 12
Turville, Henry, garden of, 6
Turville's Point, flora at, 5
Two Rivers, origin of sundae in, 77-78

University Arboretum, 13, 14
University College of Agriculture, library on beekeeping, 104

Vanderpool, Abraham, farm home, 21
Villa Louis, 17
Violet, 5, 11
Viroqua, 108

Wade House, Greenbush inn, 34
Wanona trail, 31
Water lily, 7, 11
Watertown, 48; octagonal house at, 20; early road, 35

Waukesha, railway terminal, 36
Waupun, Christmas display at, 109
Wausau, road terminal, 34; syrup making at, 100
Wayside Inn, Milwaukee saloon, 69-70
Weber, Henry, 71
Weber and Stuber's, Milwaukee restaurant and bar, 71
Welsh, houses of, 20; food, 106
Whitefish Bay, resort at, 72
Whitewater, old architecture at, 20
Whittlesey, Asaph, 42
Wild flowers, *see* Flora of Wisconsin
Wild rose, 11
Wilder, Amos P., on corsets, 48-49
Wirka, Joseph, saloon of, 74, 75
Wisconsin Dells, flora at, 6, 8, 9
Wisconsin Rapids, flora at, 6
Wisconsin River, 28, 32, 34; flora along, 9, 10; Indian travel route, 29; spellings of name, 30. *See also* Fox-Wisconsin route
Wood, Clifford, bee hunter, 104
Wood, William S., hotel proprietor, 57
Wood lily, 12
Woodland, town of, 53
Woodman, cacti at, 10; railroad to, 36
Wyalusing State Park, ferns in, 8

Yugoslavs, Christmas custom of, 108

Zick, George, bee hunter, 104
Zilisch, Ernest, 53
Zimmerman, A. G., 41
Zuebelin, Charles, 65